THE KEY GERMAN GRAMMAR

for Key Stages 3 and 4

Harriette Lanzer

Mary Glasgow Publications
An imprint of Stanley Thornes (Publishers) Ltd

Acknowledgements

The author would like to thank her father, Christian Lanzer, for his help and encouragement in writing this book.

We are grateful to the following for allowing us to reproduce copyright material:

AOK-Bundesverband
Deutsche Bahn
MVG (Medienverlagsgesellschaft MBH & Co.)

Every effort has been made to trace copyright holders but the publishers will be pleased to make the necessary arrangements at the first opportunity if there are any omissions.

First published in 1995 by:
Mary Glasgow Publications
An imprint of Stanley Thornes (Publishers) Ltd
Ellenborough House
Wellington Street
CHELTENHAM GL50 1YW
England

A catalogue record for this book is available from the British Library.

ISBN 0 7487 1923 7

99 00 / 10 9 8 7 6 5 4

Typeset by Tech-Set, Gateshead, Tyne & Wear
Printed and bound in Great Britain by Redwood Books, Trowbridge, Wiltshire

Contents

Introduction

Understanding how a language works is a vital part of learning that language. Once you can understand the grammar system, you will be able to use the language more fully and with more confidence.

If you are in your first few years of learning German and you are looking for some help in getting to grips with its grammar, then this is the book for you.

The Key to German Grammar offers you a step-by-step approach to the main grammar points you will need to know at a basic to intermediate level of German. Each section contains activities to enable you to apply the grammar you are learning. Answers are included at the back.

Use the grammar checklist quiz on page 117 to see how much grammar you already know. The answers to all those questions can be found in this book.

Key

	Handy tips to help you learn and remember the grammar
⇨ p.000	More information can be found on this page
Test your understanding	Activities after each grammar point
Hast du's kapiert?	Revision activities on the grammar points
Summary	A summary of the grammar points covered
Grammar in action	Shows you the grammar in context

Using this book

Here are a few tips for using *The Key to German Grammar*:

- Don't try to read it from cover to cover!
- Get an exercise book or a file and label it 'My Key to German Grammar'. When you learn a new grammar point, write it down. You may be able to write it in a way which is particularly easy for you to understand and remember.

- If there is a grammar point you are unsure about, or you want to learn, look it up in the contents page, turn to the relevant page in the book and work your way through the step-by-step explanations.
- As you come across new grammar points in your German lessons, look them up in this book for further help.
- Do the *Test your understanding* and *Hast du's kapiert?* exercises and check your answers in the back to see if you really have understood the explanations.
- Make learning cards for grammar points you find hard to remember. Write the explanations or the patterns on pieces of card. Keep these cards in different places. Whenever you have a spare moment, pick up the cards and test yourself on the grammar.

- Keep on revising the grammar you have learned. Note down the key points on a piece of paper and then check in this book to see if you have remembered everything correctly.
- Do try and learn some of the grammar patterns. Maybe you can think up rhymes or sentences to help you do this.
- You can learn grammar with a friend. One of you can look at this book while the other one explains the grammar point. Alternatively, the person with the book can ask the other person quiz questions on the grammar.
- Have this book in front of you when you do your written homework. You can refer to it as you go – and afterwards – to check what you are writing.
- Don't worry if you can't remember all the grammar points. You can always refer back to this book for help or ask your teacher in your next German lesson.

1 Nouns

Everything you can see, feel and hear has a name. These names are called nouns. A noun is a word for:
- a person: Jens, Anna, Freund
- a place: Bonn, Europa, Österreich
- a thing: Haus, Taxi, Kopfschmerzen
- a feeling: Mitleid, Fröhlichkeit, Gedanke.

- In German all nouns start with a capital letter: **H**amburg, **T**heater, **O**range.
- German nouns are split up into three groups: masculine nouns (m), feminine nouns (f) and neuter nouns (n).
- The three groups each have a word for 'the': ***der*** (m), ***die*** (f), ***das*** (n).
- These three groups are called genders.
- Nouns can be singular (one of something) or plural (two or more of something).
- Nouns often have small words in front of them: **der** Hund, **eine** Frau, **mein** Leben.

Grammar in action

Make a list of all the nouns in this recipe. Do you know what the nouns mean in English?

Fruchtmilch

Du brauchst dazu:
150 g Früchte (Erdbeeren oder Bananen)
¼ l Milch

So wird's gemacht:
Die Früchte mit einer Gabel auf einem flachen Teller zerdrücken.
Die Milch in einen Milchtopf geben, zerdrückte Früchte zufügen und mit einem Mixer verrühren.

☆ *Careful, not all words which start with a capital letter are nouns.*

1 *der, die, das*

A Masculine nouns (***der***)

- All masculine nouns use ***der*** for 'the': der Tag (the day), der Ball (the ball).

- Nouns to do with male people are masculine: der Mann (the man), der Lehrer (the male teacher).
- Days of the week, months, seasons and points on the compass are masculine: der Samstag (Saturday), der August (August), der Winter (the winter), der Westen (the west).
- Nouns ending in ***-ich***, ***-ig***, ***-ing***, ***-ling*** are masculine: der Frühling (the spring), der Teppich (the carpet).

B Feminine nouns (***die***)

- All feminine nouns use ***die*** for 'the': die Uhr (the watch), die Hand (the hand).
- Most words to do with female people are feminine: die Frau (the woman), die Lehrerin (the female teacher).
- Nouns ending in ***-heit***, ***-keit***, ***-ie***, ***-schaft***, ***-ung*** are feminine: die Familie (the family), die Freundschaft (the friendship).
- A lot of words ending in ***-e*** are feminine: die Karte (the map), die Pause (the break).

C Neuter nouns (***das***)

- Neuter nouns use ***das*** for 'the': das Taxi (the taxi), das Regal (the shelf).
- Nouns ending in ***-chen***, ***-lein*** are neuter: das Mädchen (the girl), das Büchlein (the little book).
- Cities, continents and most countries are neuter: das Asien (Asia), das Deutschland (Germany).

NB With many German nouns, there is no way of knowing whether they are masculine, feminine or neuter unless you learn it. So, whenever you learn a new German noun, remember to learn its gender as well.

☆ *If you're not sure about the gender of a noun, you can look it up in the dictionary.*

Fuß *m*	*the m tells you this is a masculine (**der**) word*
Hand *f*	*the f tells you this is a feminine (**die**) word*
Bein *n*	*the n tells you this is a neuter (**das**) word*

Test your understanding

Make three gender lists for these animals.

(m)	(f)	(n)
der Goldfisch	die Kuh	das Pony

die Katze	**der Hamster**	**das Pferd**
der Papagei	**das Kaninchen**	**die Schlange**
die Schildkröte	**das Krokodil**	**der Hund**

What gender are the following words? Write them out with their English meaning.

Fahrrad
das Fahrrad (n) = bicycle

a Freundin
b Mittwoch
c Österreich
d Biologie
e Honig
f Europa
g Sekretärin
h Nachbar
i Karriere

2 *ein, eine, ein*

A If you want to say 'a' instead of 'the', use ***ein***, ***eine*** or ***ein***: ein Tag (a day), eine Uhr (a watch), ein Taxi (a taxi).

B For masculine (***der***) nouns use ***ein***: ein Ball (a ball), ein Mann (a man).

C For feminine (***die***) nouns use ***eine***: eine Frau (a woman), eine Hand (a hand).

D For neuter (***das***) nouns use ***ein***: ein Regal (a shelf), ein Mädchen (a girl).

Test your understanding

Write these words with **ein, eine** or **ein**. What do they mean in English?

der Apfel   ein Apfel = an apple

a die Orange
b die Kiwi
c die Banane
d die Erdbeere
e der Pfirsich
f das Obst

3 Words made up from smaller words

A Some German words are formed by writing two shorter words together: die Schlafmatte (sleeping mat), das Taschenmesser (penknife).

B To find out whether these words are masculine, feminine or neuter, look at the last word. The gender of that last word tells you the gender of the whole word:
der Schlaf**sack** is masculine (der Sack)
die Regen**jacke** is feminine (die Jacke)
das Hand**tuch** is neuter (das Tuch).

Test your understanding

What gender are these words? What do they mean in English?

Reiseleiter (m) = travel guide

a Bettzeug
b Tischtennis
c Kleingeld
d Zahnärztin
e Fotoapparat
f Schlafanzug
g Kühlschrank

Which shorter words make up the words above? Write them out with their English meaning.

die Reise = journey; der Leiter = guide, leader

4 Plurals

A If you are talking about more than one of something, you use the plural form (pl): Heft/Hefte (book/books), Mappe/Mappen (bag/bags).

B Plurals use ***die*** for 'the'. There is no word for 'a' in the plural: die Stifte/Stifte (the pens/pens).

C German nouns have different ways of forming their plural. Most nouns add ***-e***, ***-er***, ***-(ne)n*** or ***-s*** on the end. Some nouns also add an *umlaut* (¨). Some nouns don't change in the plural.

Singular	Plural
der Filzstift	die Filzstift**e**
das Buch	die B**ü**ch**er**
der Markt	die M**ä**rkt**e**
die Pause	die Pause**n**
die Freundin	die Freundin**nen**
der Radiergummi	die Radiergummi**s**
das Auto	die Auto**s**
der Füller	die Füller

D Each time you learn a German noun with its gender, you also need to learn its plural form. In vocabulary lists, the plural form is usually given in brackets after the noun.

die Garage (n)	garage	(die Garagen)
der Garten (¨)	garden	(die Gärten)
die Gasse (n)	alley	(die Gassen)
der Gast (¨e)	guest	(die Gäste)
das Gebiet (e)	area	(die Gebiete)

☆ *You can only add an umlaut to **a** (ä), **o** (ö) and **u** (ü).*

E If you look up a word in the dictionary, you can find its plural form: **Vater** m (¨) = die Väter **Frau** f (-en) = die Frauen **Spiel** n (-e) = die Spiele.

F A lot of feminine words form their plural by adding ***-(e)n*** or ***-nen***: eine Gitarre/zwei Gitarre**n**, eine Antwort/zwei Antwort**en**, eine Ärztin/zwei Ärztin**nen**.

Test your understanding

Write out these words in the plural form.

Nachbarin f (-nen) die Nachbarin/die Nachbarinnen

a Sohn m (¨e)
b Tante f (-n)
c Mädchen n (-)
d Freund m (-e)
e Nichte f (-n)
f Kind n (-er)
g Schwiegertochter f (¨)

Use a dictionary or a vocabulary list to find out the gender and plural of the nouns overleaf.

(If the word is made up of smaller words, you need to look up the last word in the dictionary to find the gender and plural form.)

Getränk = das Getränk/die Getränke

a Szene
b Schublade
c Pickel
d Geschenk
e Jugendhaus
f Interview
g Theaterstück

5 *dieser, jeder, jener, welcher*

1 Nouns can also be used with other words which work in the same way as ***der***, ***die***, ***das***:

dieser (this)
jener (that)
jeder (every)
welcher (which)

Dieser Film ist spannend.	*This film is exciting.*
Jenes Videospiel ist doof.	*That computer game is stupid.*
Welche Disketten hast du?	*Which discs have you got?*
Jeder Computerfan ist gleich.	*Every computer fan is the same.*

Summary: Nouns

1 German nouns always start with a capital letter.

2 There are three groups (genders) of German nouns: masculine, feminine and neuter.

3 Nouns can be singular or plural.

4 There are different words for 'the' and 'a': ***der/ein*** (m), ***die/eine*** (f), ***das/ein*** (n), ***die*** (pl).

5 Some German words are made up from two or more smaller words. The gender and plural of these words are taken from the last word of the long word.

6 Plural forms need to be learned individually or looked up in the dictionary – there are many variations.

Read the following passage. Make four lists of the nouns: masculine, feminine, neuter, plural.

Die Familie Gramm wohnt in einem großen Schloß in Deutschland. Es gibt zwei Kinder in der Familie – Gramma und Grimmi. Sie sind beide sechzehn Jahre alt. Sie gehen nicht in die Schule. Sie lernen alles von ihren Eltern, Graf und Gräfin Gramm. Bei dieser Familie ist immer was los – Partys im Schwimmbad, Feste in der Rollschuhdisco disco und Spiele im Keller. Gramma und Grimmi haben viele Freunde, und sie finden das Leben nie langweilig.

Write these words out in the columns.

The	A	Plural	English
der Pulli	ein Pulli	die Pullis	jumper(s)

das Kleid	**die Socke**	**das Hemd**
der Mantel	**der Rock**	**das T-Shirt**
die Krawatte	**der Anzug**	**die Hose**

Which of the following words is the odd one out each time? Can you explain why?

a Micha Kino Hamburg ein Kai
b Mutter Briefträger Schwester Freundin Pilotin
c Auto Fähre Schiff Fahrrad Flugzeug
d Arm Finger Hand Fuß Magen
e Banane Champignons Tomaten Äpfel Birnen
f Magenschmerzen Taschengeld Phantasie Nachttisch Fußball

- *When you learn a noun for the first time, learn its gender and plural form as well.*
- *Write the noun down if you keep having to look it up.*
- *You could colour code nouns for the different genders in your vocabulary book.*

2 Cases

- Cases give you information about the words in a sentence. You can often recognise a case from a change in the **der** or **ein** word.
- The sentences below show you examples of different cases:

Der Mann steht neben **der** Tür.	*The man is standing next to the door.*
Es gibt **eine** Frau mit **dem** Mann.	*There is a woman with the man.*
Die Frau trägt **einen** Mantel.	*The woman is wearing a coat.*
Der Mann spricht mit **der** Frau.	*The man is talking with the woman.*

- There are three main cases in German: nominative (nom), accusative (acc) and dative (dat).
- There is also a fourth case, genitive (gen), but this is not used as much in spoken German.
- This table shows you how the words for ***der*, *die*, *das*** change in the different cases.

	m	f	n	pl
Nom	der	die	das	die
Acc	**den**	die	das	die
Dat	**dem**	**der**	**dem**	**den**
Gen	**des**	**der**	**des**	**der**

☆ *Try and learn these changes. They are very important for German grammar.*

- ***dieser*** (this), ***jener*** (that), ***jeder*** (every), ***welcher*** (which) all have the same changes as this table.

Grammar in action

Taschengeld-Paß:

Die Trumpfkarte für alle zwischen 12 und 17 Jahren: Mit dem Taschengeld-Paß kostet die Schiene überall nur die Hälfte. Im gesamten Bundesbahn- und Reichsbahn-Netz. Und in den meisten Regional-Bussen der örtlichen Verkehrsgesellschaften – ja sogar im ICE. Ein ganzes Jahr lang.

Den extrastarken Taschengeld-Paß gibt es schon für DM 40,–

The words below are all in different cases in the text on page 9. Find them in the text and then find the ***der/die/das*** words in the table on page 9.

die Trumpfkarte (f/nom)
dem Taschengeld-Paß (m/dat)
die Schiene (f/nom)
die Hälfte (f/nom)
den meisten Regionalbussen (pl/dat)
der örtlichen Verkehrsgesellschaften (pl/gen)

1 Nominative case (subject)

A When you learn a word or look it up in the dictionary, you will find the nominative case:
der Mann (m), die Frau (f), das Kind (n), die Schmerzen (pl).

B You use the nominative case for the subject of the sentence. That is the person or thing doing the action of the verb.

Der Hund beißt den Mann.

Die Briefträgerin sieht das Ungeheuer.

Das Mädchen ißt eine Orange.

Die Kinder werfen die Bälle.

C To find the subject in a sentence, first of all find the verb (the doing word). Then ask yourself, 'Who or what is doing the verb?' That will be the subject (in the nominative case).

D The subject is not always the word at the beginning of the sentence:

Am Montag kommt **der Bus** nicht.	*The bus doesn't come on Monday.*
Leider habe **ich** kein Geld.	*Unfortunately I haven't got any money.*

E These are the nominative case words for 'the':

	m	f	n	pl
Nom	der	die	das	die

Test your understanding

Find the subject of the following sentences.

Breite **Hosen** sind modisch.

a Kühe fressen Gras.
b Sprechen Sie Deutsch?
c Das Brot liegt auf dem Tisch.
d Heute bringt der Briefträger keine Post für mich.
e Der Kaffee in diesem Restaurant schmeckt furchtbar.
f Wo finde ich die Taschen und die Regenschirme?
g Um acht Uhr beginnt die Schule wieder.

Make up sentences using the pictures below as the subject each time. How many sentences can you think of for each item (use a different verb each time)?

Das Auto ist in der Garage. Das Haus sieht schön aus .....

   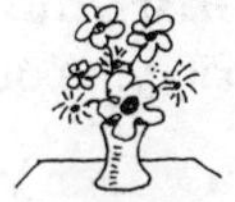

2 Accusative case (object)

A Only the masculine word for 'the' changes in the accusative case: ***der Freund*** becomes ***den Freund***.

B You use the accusative case for the person or thing having something done to them by the subject of the sentence. This person or thing is called the direct object.

Der Mann beißt **den Hund**.

Das Ungeheuer jagt **die Briefträgerin**.

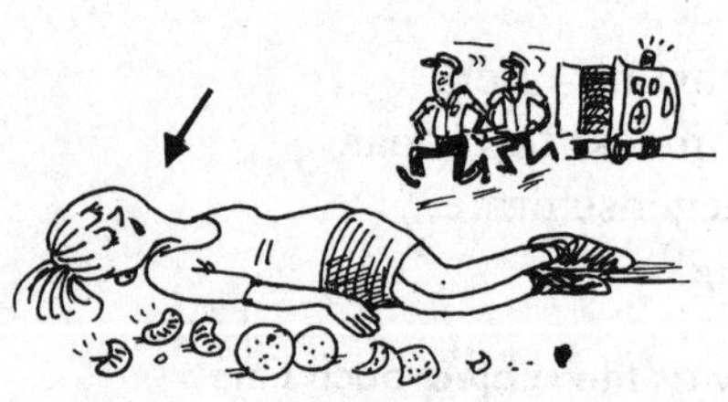

Die Orange vergiftet **das Mädchen**.

Die Bälle treffen **die Nachbarn**.

C To find the direct object in a sentence, find the verb. Then ask yourself, 'Who or what is having the verb done to them?'

D Some prepositions are followed by the accusative case (⇨ p.20).

E This table shows you the nominative and accusative words for 'the':

	m	f	n	pl
Nom	der	die	das	die
Acc	**den**	die	das	die

Test your understanding ▾▾

Find the object in these sentences.

a Der Verrückte schmeißt den Teller zum Boden.
b Siehst du den Kerl da hinten?

c Die Touristen besuchen immer den Dom.
d Die Römer haben die Sehenswürdigkeiten gebaut.
e Gestern habe ich die ganze Familie besucht.
f Den Film finde ich wunderbar.
g Die Direktorin hat die Kinder nicht gern.

▲▲

3 Dative case

A All the words for 'the' change in the dative case: ***der*** (m) = ***dem***, ***die*** (f) = ***der***, ***das*** (n) = ***dem***, ***die*** (pl) = ***den***.

B You use the dative case for the person or thing having something done *to* them. This person or thing is called the indirect object of the sentence.

Der Elefant gibt **dem Schüler** eine Blume.

Die Schülerin zeigt **der Lehrerin** ihre Tätowierung.

Der Arzt schickt **dem Mädchen** sein Herz.

Das Ungeheuer bringt **den Kindern** ein Geschenk.

C Some verbs are followed by the dative case:

bringen	(to bring [to])
danken	(to thank)
erzählen	(to tell [to])
folgen	(to follow)
geben	(to give [to])
helfen	(to help)

reichen	(to pass [to])
sagen	(to say [to])
schicken	(to send [to])
zeigen	(to show [to])

The dative case is also used in English, but we often hide it: I give a book **to** the teacher/I give the teacher a book.

D Some prepositions are followed by the dative case (⇨ p.20).

E This table shows you the nominative, accusative and dative words for 'the':

	m	f	n	pl
Nom	der	die	das	die
Acc	den	die	das	die
Dat	**dem**	**der**	**dem**	**den**

Test your understanding

Fill in the gaps with the dative.

a Er bringt ..... Freundin ein Erdbeereis.
b Reichst du bitte ..... Gast ein Handtuch?
c Hilfst du bitte ..... müden Kellner?
d Morgen schicke ich ..... Großeltern eine Postkarte.
e Er sagt ..... Lehrer: »Diese Mathestunde ist so-o langweilig.«
f ..... alten Frau hilft er nicht.

4 Genitive case

A The genitive case is hardly used in spoken German but is often found in written German.

B All the words for 'the' change in the genitive case: ***der*** (m) = ***des***, ***die*** (f) = ***der***, ***das*** (n) = ***des***, ***die*** (pl) = ***der***.

C The genitive case translates 'of' the/my, etc. You use it to talk about who or what things belong to. In German, you say 'the car of my father' (not 'my father's car').

das Auto **des Vaters**	*the father's car*
die Arbeit **der Mutter**	*the mother's work*
das Spiel **des Kindes**	*the child's game*
die Spiele **der Kinder**	*the children's games*

☆ *If you are using the genitive with a name, you can simply say* ***Gabis Schwester***, ***Peters Onkel****, etc. You don't need an apostrophe before the* ***s****.*

D In the masculine and neuter genitive forms, you have to add ***-(e)s*** to the end of the noun:

die Uhr des Manne**s** — *the man's watch*
die Hütte des Kaninchen**s** — *the rabbit's hutch*

E This table shows you the nominative, accusative, dative and genitive words for 'the':

	m	f	n	pl
Nom	der	die	das	die
Acc	den	die	das	die
Dat	dem	der	dem	den
Gen	**des**	**der**	**des**	**der**

Test your understanding

Make up sentences using the genitive with the following words.

das Kaninchen/Karottensuppe

Das Lieblingsessen des Kaninchens ist Karottensuppe.

a die Katzen/Milchpudding
b der Hund/Schokosoße
c die Maus/Käsebrot
d das Pferd/Müsli

Describe the things these people have got.

Das Mädchen hat einen neuen Ball. Der Ball des Mädchens ist neu.

a Der Fahrer hat ein schnelles Auto.
b Die Lehrerin trägt eine altmodische Bluse.
c Der Star hat einen dummen Schnurrbart.
d Die Kinder essen leckere Kekse.

5 Case changes with *ein, kein, mein .....*

A It is not only ***der***, ***die***, ***das*** that change with cases. Other words such as ***ein***, ***mein***, ***kein***, ***dein***, etc. change as well.

B This table shows you how these words change:

	m	f	n	pl
Nom	mein	meine	mein	meine
Acc	**meinen**	meine	mein	meine
Dat	**meinem**	**meiner**	**meinem**	**meinen**
(Gen	meines	meiner	meines	meiner)

c The changes are very similar to **der**, **die**, **das** (⇨ p.9).

Ich sehe d**en**/ein**en** Mann.	*I see the/a man.*
Wir finden di**e**/dein**e** Zeitschrift toll.	*We like the/your magazine.*
Hilfst du bitte d**en**/ihr**en** Kindern.	*Please help the/her children.*

Test your understanding

Replace 'the' with the word in brackets.

Kaufst du mir bitte die Torte? (ein)   Kaufst du mir bitte eine Torte?

a Ich gehe mit dem Meerschweinchen spazieren. (mein)
b Gehst du zu der Strandparty? (ein)
c Die Kinder sind so frech. (ihr)
d Die Programme sind stinklangweilig. (dein)
e Gestern sahen wir den Hamster im Garten. (kein)
f Die Kekse schmecken lecker. (sein)
g Wo ist hier die Toilette? (ein)

Summary: Cases

1 There are four cases in German: nominative, accusative, dative and genitive.

2 Cases give you information about the sentence. They tell you what role a word plays in a sentence.

3 The nominative case is used for the subject of the sentence.

4 The accusative case is used for the direct object and after certain prepositions.

5 The dative case is used for the indirect object and after certain prepositions.

6 The genitive case is not used much in spoken German, but it indicates belonging to someone.

7 Cases change words for 'the' and other words such as ***ein***, ***mein***, ***kein***.

8 The case table on page 9 needs to be learned as the cases are used in nearly every German sentence.

☆ ***If you know the case table, you will be able to make sense of sentences more easily.***

Hast du's kapiert?

Fill in the gaps with a suitable word, such as 'a', 'my', 'your', 'the' etc.

☆ *Look at the noun each time and say what gender (m, f, n) it is or if it's plural. Then ask yourself what case it is. You can then use the case table (or your memory!) to choose the correct word.*

a Ich habe ..... neue Freundin. Sie heißt Grisilde.

b ..... Name ist Oma Gramm.

c Wo ist ..... Mann? Ich habe ..... Hut für ihn.

d Igitt. Grisilde stinkt! Und sie trägt so ..... blöden Rock.

e ..... Katze ..... Tochter hat ..... Briefträger im Gesicht gekratzt.

Answer these questions.

a Was gibt es auf deinem Tisch? – Es gibt einen Stift, ...
b Was trägst du zur Schule? – Ich trage .....
c Mit wem wohnst du? – Ich wohne mit meiner Mutter, ...
d Welche Haustiere hättest du gern? – Ich hätte gern .....

Translate these sentences.

a I help the doctor.
b The girl tells the children a story.
c The boy thanks the policewoman.
d My sister shows her photos to the class.
e Can you pass the salt to the guest?
f We give the cats some chocolate.
g We show the child our map.

Can you say the case table from page 9 without looking at it?

3 *Prepositions*

- A preposition is a short word which tells you about where something is, or is going to:

auf dem Tisch	*on the table*
durch die Tür	*through the door*
unter dem Bett	*under the bed*
ins Klassenzimmer	*into the classroom*

- A preposition can also tell you about the time:

um sechs Uhr	*at six o'clock*
nach der Schule	*after school*
am Freitag	*on Friday*
im Dezember	*in December*

- A preposition gives you more information about things:

mit dem Hund	*with the dog*
von meiner Freundin	*from my friend*
ohne meine Jacke	*without my jacket*

- Most prepositions are followed by either the accusative or the dative case. This means that words such as ***der***, ***ein***, ***mein*** change (⇨ pp.9 and 15).

Grammar in action

Can you find six prepositions in this text?
What do they mean in English?

> Viele Wege führen nach Hellabrunn. Die U-Bahn-Linie 3 bis Station Thalkirchen. Bus 52 ab Stadtmitte Marienplatz. Für Autofahrer ist auf dem Mittleren Ring die Route beschildert. Parkplätze gegenüber den Eingängen.

1 Cases with prepositions

A This diagram shows the German prepositions used with the accusative and/or dative case.

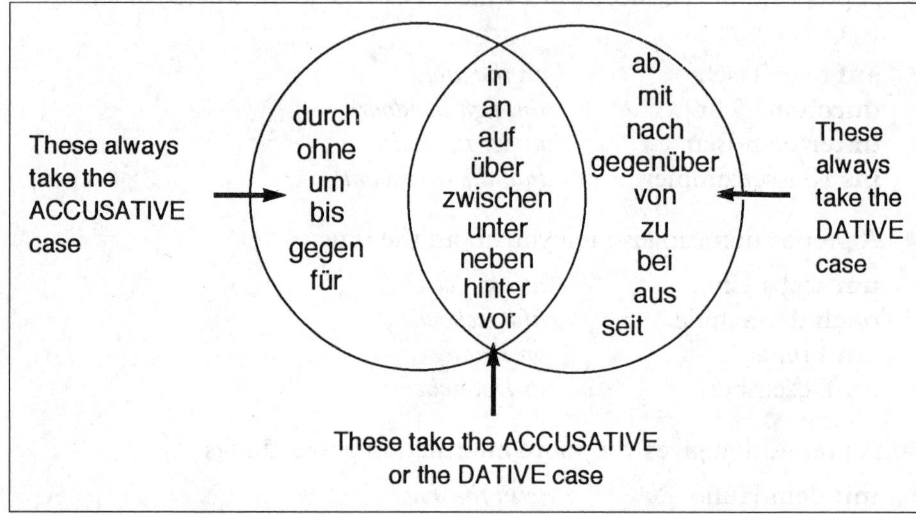

☆ *When you learn a preposition, learn the case it takes at the same time. To make this easier, you could make up a sentence with the first letter of each preposition in a group, e.g. for accusative prepositions: Did Our Ugly Brother Get Fired?*

B Accusative case prepositions:

durch (through)
ohne (without)
um (at; around)
bis (until)
gegen (against)
für (for)

C Dative case prepositions:

ab (from)
aus (out of)
bei (at the home of/near)
gegenüber (opposite)
mit (with)

nach (after)
seit (since)
von (from)
zu (to)

D A few prepositions are followed by the genitive case:

trotz (in spite of)
während (during)
wegen (because of)

Test your understanding

Find a suitable preposition for each gap.

a Der Ball fliegt ..... das Fenster und landet gerade dort.
b Fährst du ..... deiner Klasse in die Schweiz?
c Wie weit ist es ..... deiner Wohnung ..... meinem Büro?
d Ich kaufe ein Geschenk ..... meinen Stiefbruder.
e Geh ..... die Ecke und dann links.
f Sie nimmt eine Fahrkarte ..... der Tasche.
g ..... acht Uhr komme ich vorbei.

Choose the correct word for each sentence.

a Ich gehe mit dem/den Hund spazieren.
b Wir gehen durch den/dem Park.
c Nach der/die Schule treffe ich mich mit meiner/meine Freundin.
d Heute gehe ich ohne einen/ein Pulli in die Stadt.
e Bei meinen/meine Großeltern ist es immer sehr schön.
f Was hast du von deinem/deinen Vater zum Geburtstag bekommen?
g Geh aus der/die Tür und gleich links.

2 Accusative or dative prepositions

A These prepositions can take either the accusative or the dative case:

an (on; at; up to)
auf (on top of)
hinter (behind)
in (in, into)
neben (next to)
über (over)

unter (under)
vor (in front of; before)
zwischen (between)

NB When **vor** means 'before', it always takes the dative case.

B If there is movement towards a place, these prepositions take the accusative case:

Wo fliegt Fritz hin? Fritz fliegt .....

C If there is no movement towards a place, they take the dative case:
Wo bleibt Fritz? Fritz bleibt .....

D If there is movement within a restricted area, the prepositions take the dative case:

Die Katze läuft in **das** Zimmer.	*The cat is running into the room.*
Die Katze läuft in **dem** Zimmer.	*The cat is running in* (i.e. around) *the room.*

Test your understanding

Choose the correct word in the following sentences. Is the answer accusative or dative?

a Der Ball ist in der/die Tasche (f).
b Wir spielen Tennis auf dem/den Spielplatz (m).
c Kommst du mit in die/der Konditorei (f)?
d Mein Skateboard ist noch unter meinem/mein Bett (n).
e Ich komme nicht über die/der Mauer (f).
f Wir treffen euch vor der/die Schule (f).
g Unser Haus ist hinter dem/das Geschäft (n).

Complete the following sentences, putting the words into the accusative or the dative case.

Ich stelle einen Teller auf den Tisch.
Jetzt gibt es einen Teller auf dem Tisch.

das Regal	**die Tasche**	**die Wand**	**das Bett**
	das Kino	**die Bäckerei**	

a Ich lege die Bücher auf .....
Jetzt sind die Bücher auf .....
b Ich stecke das Geld in .....
Jetzt ist das Geld in .....
c Ich hange das Bild an .....
Jetzt hängt das Bild an .....
d Der Hund kriecht unter .....
Jetzt schläft der Hund unter .....

e Sie läuft vor .....
Er wartet vor .....
f Ich arbeite in .....
Jeden Tag gehe ich in .....

▲▲▲

3 Shortening words with prepositions

A Some prepositions join with ***das***, ***dem***, ***der*** to make one word:

in das – ins
in dem – im
an das – ans
an dem – am
auf das – aufs
bei dem – beim
von dem – vom
zu dem – zum
zu der – zur

Ich gehe **zur** Post.	*I go to the post office.*
Er ist **im** Kino.	*He's in the cinema.*
Sie ist **beim** Arzt.	*She's at the doctor.*

B The prepositions below also join together to make one word. Some of them add an ***r*** in the middle.

damit (with it/them)
dafür (for it/them)
dagegen (against it/them)
darauf (on it/them)
darunter (under it/them)

Spielst du **damit**?	*Are you playing with it?*
Ich sitze **darunter**.	*I'm sitting under it.*
Er kämpft **dagegen**.	*He's fighting against it.*

Test your understanding

Was macht man mit einem Kuli? Man schreibt damit.

Was macht man mit .....

a Messer und Gabel?
b einem Computer?
c den Augen?
d einem Ball?

sieht	spielt	ißt	arbeitet

4 Phrases with prepositions

A Some prepositions have different meanings when they are used in set phrases like the ones below.

Ich gehe **nach Hause**. Ich sitze **zu Hause**.	*I'm going home.* *I'm sitting at home.*
Bei uns ist immer was los.	*There's always something going on at our house.*
Bei gutem Wetter spielen wir draußen.	*In good weather we play outside.*
Fahren wir **mit dem Auto**? Nein, wir gehen **zu Fuß**.	*Are we going by car?* *No, we're going on foot.*
Ich wohne **auf dem Land**. Wir fahren **aufs Land**. Ich fahre **ins Ausland**. Mein Freund wohnt **im Ausland**.	*I live in the country.* *We're going to the countryside.* *I'm going abroad.* *My friend lives abroad.*
Wie heißt das **auf deutsch**?	*What's that called in German?*
Ich gehe **auf die Uni**.	*I go to university.*
Zu Ostern/Weihnachten. Fünf Briefmarken **zu einer Mark**, bitte.	*At Easter/Christmas.* *Five one mark stamps please.*

Summary: Prepositions

1 Prepositions are small words which give information about time, place and actions.

2 There are three main groups of prepositions:

- always followed by the accusative
- always followed by the dative
- followed by the accusative (where movement is involved) or the dative (where no movement is involved).

3 Some prepositions join with ***der***, ***die***, ***das*** to make one word.

Describe the flat after Gramma and Grimmi have tidied it up:

Das Radio ist in der Küche .....

Heute räumen Gramma und Grimmi bei Oma Gramm auf. Leider kommt alles in die falschen Zimmer. Das Radio kommt in die Küche, die Töpfe kommen ins Schlafzimmer, die Kleider kommen ins Wohnzimmer und der Fernseher kommt ins Badezimmer. Gramma stellt das Geschirr in den Flur und die Blumen in die Garage. Grimmi legt die Brille seiner Oma in den Kühlschrank!
»Das nächste Mal werde ich alleine aufräumen«, sagt Oma Gramm.
»Gott sei Dank«, sagen Grimmi und Gramma.

Answer these questions with a preposition each time.

a Wo sieht man einen Film?
b Womit ißt man Spaghetti?
c Wann gehst du nicht in die Schule?
d Was kann man in deiner Stadt machen?
e Wo liegt dein Haus?
f Wohin gehst du gern am Wochenende?
g An wen schreibst du oft?

4 Adjectives

- Adjectives describe nouns. They can be words for:
  - colours: rot, gelb, blau
  - sizes: groß, klein, kurz
  - moods: traurig, lustig, böse
  - weather: kalt, warm, regnerisch
  - opinions: toll, langweilig, interessant
  - characteristics: freundlich, hilfsbereit, pünktlich

- Adjectives often have opposites:

schnell/langsam	(fast/slow)
heiß/kalt	(hot/cold)
pünktlich/unpünktlich	(punctual/unpunctual)
glücklich/traurig	(happy/sad)
dick/dünn	(fat/thin)
lang/kurz	(long/short)
alt/jung	(old/young)
gut/schlecht	(good/bad)

- You can use adjectives after a noun:

Das Kaninchen ist **verrückt**.	*The rabbit is crazy.*
Diese Mützen sehen **schrecklich** aus.	*These hats look terrible.*

- You can use adjectives before a noun. The adjective then needs an ending:

das **verrückte** Kaninchen	*the crazy rabbit*
diese **schrecklichen** Mützen	*these terrible hats*

Grammar in action
**Make a list of adjectives from this letter.
Which one has got an ending?**

aus Mannheim

HÜBSCH, BLOND UND IMMER NOCH KEINEN FREUND

Ich bin hübsch und blond – und das ist mein Problem. Die meisten Leute denken nämlich, nur weil ich so aussehe, hätte ich ganz viele Freunde und sei angeberisch. So bin ich überhaupt nicht. Ich bin nett, freundlich, hilfsbereit, und ich hatte noch nie einen Freund. Wenn die anderen das hören, sagen sie immer: „Was? Du? Du bist doch so hübsch mit deinen blonden Haaren!"

1 Adjectives with *der, die, das*

A If you use an adjective before a noun and after ***der***, ***die***, ***das***, you need to add ***-e*** or ***-en*** to the adjective.

B This chart shows you the endings:

	m	f
Nom	der rot**e** Pulli	die rot**e** Bluse
Acc	den rot**en** Pulli	die rot**e** Bluse
Dat	dem rot**en** Pulli	der rot**en** Bluse
Gen	des rot**en** Pullis	der rot**en** Bluse

	n	pl
Nom	das rot**e** Hemd	die rot**en** Socken
Acc	das rot**e** Hemd	die rot**en** Socken
Dat	dem rot**en** Hemd	den rot**en** Socken
Gen	des rot**en** Hemdes	der rot**en** Socken

C You also use those endings after ***dieser*** (this), ***jener*** (that), ***jeder*** (each), ***mancher*** (some), ***alle*** (all) and ***welcher*** (which).

D The endings make the adjective match the noun it is describing.

Der blau**e** Pullover gefällt mir nicht.	*I don't like the blue pullover.*
Ich mag die grün**e** Jacke.	*I like the green jacket.*
Was liegt unter den schmutzig**en** Socken?	*What's under the dirty socks?*
Das schwarz**e** Hemd paßt dir gut.	*The black shirt fits you well.*

Test your understanding

Write these sentences with the adjective before the noun.

Die Straße ist lang = die lange Straße

a Der Tunnel ist neu.
b Das Wetter ist scheußlich.
c Die Erwachsenen sind wahnsinnig.
d Diese Autobahnstrecke ist stinklangweilig.
e Alle Österreicher sind freundlich.
f Jede Sprache ist interessant.
g Welche Witze sind gemein?

2 Adjectives with *ein, mein, dein .....*

A If you use an adjective before a noun and after **ein**, **kein**, **mein**, etc. you need to add **-e**, **-er**, **-en** or **-es** to the adjective.

B This chart shows you the endings:

	m	f
Nom	ein rot**er** Pulli	eine rot**e** Bluse
Acc	einen rot**en** Pulli	eine rot**e** Bluse
Dat	einem rot**en** Pulli	einer rot**en** Bluse
Gen	eines rot**en** Pullis	einer rot**en** Bluse

	n	pl
Nom	ein rot**es** Hemd	meine rot**en** Socken
Acc	ein rot**es** Hemd	meine rot**en** Socken
Dat	einem rot**en** Hemd	meinen rot**en** Socken
Gen	eines rot**en** Hemdes	meiner rot**en** Socken

C You also use those endings after ***dein*** (your), ***sein*** (his/its), ***ihr/Ihr*** (her/their, your), ***unser*** (our), ***euer*** (your).

☆ *Look at the adjective chart for **der**, **die**, **das** on p.29. Look at how many endings are the same for **der** and **ein** words. That will help you learn the endings more quickly.*

D The endings make the adjective match the noun it is describing.

Dein blau**er** Pulli gefällt mir gut.	*I like your blue pullover.*
Ich mag seine grün**e** Jacke.	*I like his green jacket.*
Was liegt unter ihren schmutzig**en** Socken?	*What's under her dirty socks?*
Ein schwarz**es** Hemd steht dir gut.	*A black shirt suits you.*

Test your understanding ▼▼▼
Write the following sentences out with the correct form of the adjective.

Ich möchte einen Kuli (rot). Ich möchte einen roten Kuli.

a Ich möchte eine Kassette (toll).
b Ich habe einen Teller (bunt).
c Das ist ein Computer (gut).
d Ist das deine Uhr (neu)?
e Siehst du seine Kinder (jung)?
f Gibt es ein Programm (interessant) heute abend?
g Du bist ein Junge (furchtbar).

▲▲

3 Adjectives on their own

A If you use an adjective without an article (i.e without ***ein***, ***der***, ***alle***, etc.), you need to add ***-e***, ***-er***, ***-em***, ***-en*** or ***-es*** to the adjective.

B This chart shows you the endings:

	m	f	n	pl
Nom	rot**er** Pulli	rot**e** Bluse	rot**es** Hemd	rot**e** Socken
Acc	rot**en** Pulli	rot**e** Bluse	rot**es** Hemd	rot**e** Socken
Dat	rot**em** Pulli	rot**er** Bluse	rot**em** Hemd	rot**en** Socken
(Gen	rot**en** Pullis	rot**er** Bluse	rot**en** Hemdes	rot**er** Socken)

C You also use those endings after a number: ***hundert blaue Socken***.

☆ *Look at the **der/die/das** chart on p.9. The adjective endings on page 31 (apart from the genitive) are the same.*

D The endings make the adjective match the noun it is describing.

Zwei blau**e** Pullis, bitte.	*Two blue jumpers, please.*
Grün**e** Jacken stehen mir nicht.	*Green jackets don't suit me.*
Warum hast du drei schwarz**e** Socken?	*Why have you got three black socks?*

Test your understanding

Write labels for this picture.

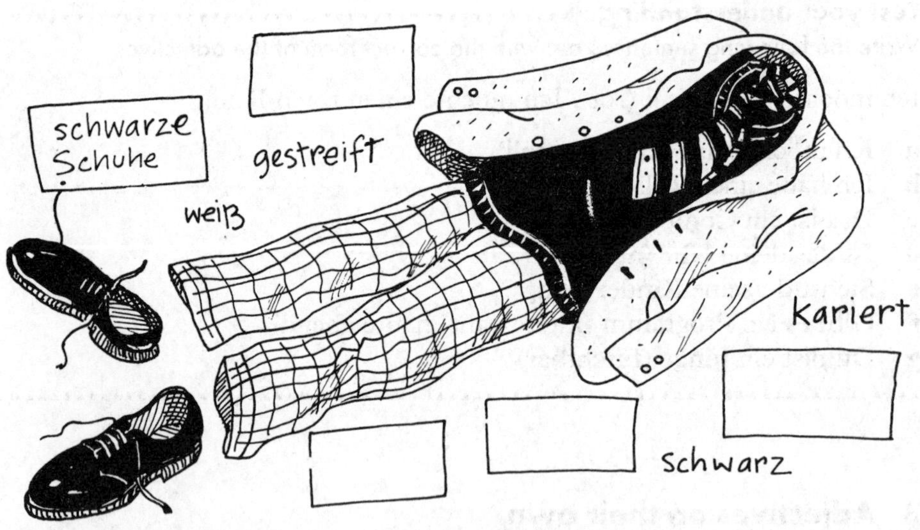

4 Comparing things

A If you want to say something is bigger, heavier, more interesting than something else, you need to use the comparative form of the adjective.

B In German, the comparative form is quite similar to English – you usually add **-er** to the end of the adjective:

klein/klein**er**	(small/smaller)
bunt/bunt**er**	(colourful/more colourful)
furchtbar/furchtbar**er**	(terrible/more terrible)

C The German word for 'than' in the comparative is ***als***.

Florian ist netter **als** Franz.	*Florian is nicer than Franz.*
Biologie ist interessanter **als** Sport.	*Biology is more interesting than sport.*

D There are some adjectives which add an *umlaut* as well as **-er** in the comparative.

groß/gr**ö**ßer	(big/bigger)
alt/**ä**lter	(old/older)
hart/h**ä**rter	(hard/harder)
jung/j**ü**nger	(young/younger)
kurz/k**ü**rzer	(short/shorter)
lang/l**ä**nger	(long/longer)
warm/w**ä**rmer	(warm/warmer)
kalt/k**ä**lter	(cold/colder)

E There are three important adjectives which have irregular comparatives.

gut/besser	(good/better)
hoch/höher	(high/higher)
viel/mehr	(many/more)

F If you want to say something is '(not) as ..... as' something else, you say ***(nicht) so ..... wie***.

Ich bin **so** dick **wie** du.	*I'm as fat as you.*
August ist **so** warm **wie** Juli.	*August is as warm as July.*
Deutschland ist nicht **so** groß **wie** China.	*Germany is not as big as China.*
Er ist nicht **so** intelligent **wie** ich.	*He's not as clever as I am.*

Test your understanding ▼▼

Find the opposites:

leicht	**alt**	**schnell**	**einfach**	**kurz**	**faul**
schwer	**billig**	**lang**	**groß**	**langsam**	
schwierig	**fleißig**	**klein**	**jung**	**teuer**	

Use the adjectives above to compare the statements in the sentences below. There are two answers to each one.

Oma ist 62, und Opa ist 65.
Oma ist jünger als Opa. Opa ist älter als Oma.

a Bonbons kosten drei Mark. Schokolade kostet zwei Mark.
b Karl wiegt 50 Kilo. Margit wiegt 47 Kilo.
c Der Kuli ist 35 cm lang. Der Stift ist 30 cm lang.
d Dirks Auto fährt 100 km pro Stunde. Gabis Auto fährt 150 km pro Stunde.
e Birgit ist fleißig. Jörg ist nicht sehr fleißig.
f Mathe ist einfach. Geschichte ist sehr einfach.
g Felix ist 1 Meter 60 groß. Eleni ist 1 Meter 50 groß.

Think of a word for each of the categories below. Then find out what your partner's words are. Compare the two words each time.

Ich finde Sport interessanter als Musik.

	Ich	Partner(in)
interessantes Fach	Sport	Musik
gutes Buch		
schöne Farbe		
langweiliges Programm		
dummes Hobby		
tolle Stadt		
schwierige Sprache		
.....		

▲▲

5 Superlative adjectives (the biggest, fastest .....)

A If you want to say something is the biggest, heaviest, funniest, etc. you need to use the superlative form of the adjective.

B In German you usually add ***-(e)ste*** to the end of the adjective to form the superlative:

streng/streng**ste** (strict/strictest)
toll/toll**ste** (great/greatest)
billig/billig**ste** (cheap/cheapest)

C There are some adjectives which add an *umlaut* as well as ***-(e)ste*** in the superlative:

alt/**ä**lteste (old/oldest)
groß/gr**ö**ßte (big/biggest)
jung/j**ü**ngste (younger/youngest)
hart/h**ä**rteste (hard/hardest)
hoch/h**ö**chste (high/highest)
kurz/k**ü**rzeste (short/shortest)
lang/l**ä**ngste (long/longest)
warm/w**ä**rmste (warm/warmest)
kalt/k**ä**lteste (cold/coldest)

☆ *Compare this list to the one on p.33. They are very similar.*

D There are two important adjectives which have irregular superlatives:

gut/beste (good/best)
viel/meiste (many/most)

E When you use the superlative before a noun, it works just like an ordinary adjective (⇨ p.29):

mein bester Freund — *my best friend*
die schönsten Geschichten — *the nicest stories*
das billigste Ding — *the cheapest thing*

F You can use the superlatives with a verb as in the examples below:

Sie läuft am schnellsten. — *She runs fastest of all/the fastest.*
Er kocht am besten. — *He cooks the best.*
Sie fahren am langsamsten. — *They drive the slowest.*

G Here are a couple of expressions which are useful to remember:

Am liebsten spiele ich Golf. — *I like golf best.*
Höchstens kostet es 1000 Mark. — *At the most, it will cost 1000 marks.*

Test your understanding

Make up sentences about these pictures using the words given below.

Das langsamste Tier ist eine Schnecke.

der Berg/Everest

der Fluß/der Nil

das Wort

das Tier/der Gepard

die Münze

hoch	**lang**	**klein**	**schnell**	**kurz**

Can you think of any more things which are the fastest, slowest, etc? Make up sentences to describe them.

Das höchste Gebäude in unserer Stadt ist .....
Der längste Tag des Jahres ist .....

Summary: Adjectives

1. Adjectives are used to describe nouns.
2. You can use an adjective after a noun.
3. If you use an adjective before a noun it needs an ending.
4. You can compare things with adjectives.

☆ ***When you learn an adjective, try and learn its opposite at the same time.***

Hast du's kapiert?

Answer the questions below using the comparative.

- **a** Was ist schwieriger – Deutsch oder Englisch? Deutsch ist schwieriger als .....
- **b** Was ist interessanter – Zeitschriften oder Zeitungen?
- **c** Was ist schlimmer – Kopfschmerzen oder Magenschmerzen?
- **d** Was schmeckt leckerer – Bohnen oder Kaugummi?
- **e** Was ist langweiliger – Montag oder Samstag?
- **f** Was ist wichtiger – Geld oder Freundschaft?
- **g** Was ist süßer – Hunde oder Katzen?

Make up sentences using an adjective and a noun from the words given.
Deine rote Hose ist total altmodisch.

rot **gut** **interessant** **fantastisch** **traurig**	**der Mann** **Geschichten** **das Fach** **das Buch** **der Film** **Haustiere**

Complete the text below putting the right endings on the adjectives.

groß	beste	lecker	modisch	schön
häßlich	kariert	neu	gut	freundlich

Heute gibt es eine ..... Party bei uns. Ich habe meine ..... Freunde und Freundinnen eingeladen. Ich habe eine ..... Torte gemacht. Sie ist aus Bananen und Rosinen. Zur Party trage ich eine ..... Hose und eine ..... Bluse.

Natürlich müssen Grimmi und seine ..... Freundin zur Party kommen. Hoffentlich trägt er seine .... Hose nicht.

Ich habe eine ..... Kassette für die Party gekauft. Es gibt aber leider nur ein ..... Lied darauf! Wir können aber selber singen und Musik machen. Das wird sicher unsere ..... Nachbarn freuen!

5 Personal pronouns

- Pronouns are small words which refer to people and things. You use them instead of repeating the noun: ***sie*** (she), ***wir*** (we), ***ihr*** (you), ***es*** (it).

- If you use a personal pronoun, you don't have to repeat people's names:

Gregor fährt in die Stadt.	*Gregor goes to town.*
Er besucht seinen Freund.	*He visits his friend.*
Hans besucht Kai und Margit.	*Hans is visiting Kai and Margit.*
Er mag **sie** sehr.	*He likes them a lot.*

- Like ***der***, ***die***, ***das*** (⇨ p.9) the words for the German pronouns change in the accusative and dative case.

- This chart shows you the pronouns and how they change:

	I	you	he	she	it	we	you/they	you
Nom	ich	du	er	sie	es	wir	Sie/sie	ihr
Acc	mich	dich	ihn	sie	es	uns	Sie/sie	euch
Dat	mir	dir	ihm	ihr	ihm	uns	Ihnen/ihnen	euch

Grammar in action

How many pronouns can you find in this slogan?
What does the slogan mean?

Für Ihre Gesundheit
machen wir
uns stark.

1 *ich, du, er .....*

A The chart below shows you when to use the personal pronouns.

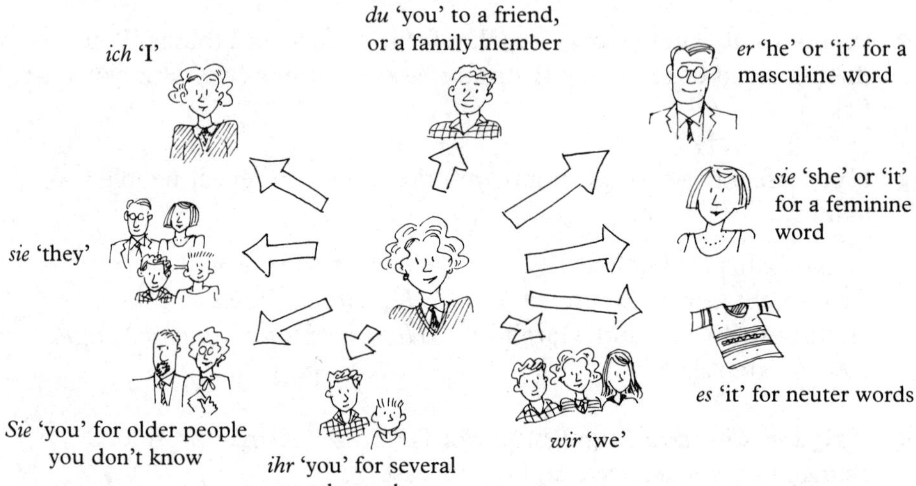

B All these pronouns are in the nominative case. They refer to the subject of the sentence, i.e. the person doing the action of the verb (⇨ p.10).

Wir lachen über den Witz.	*We laugh about the joke.*
Gestern **ist er** Millionär geworden.	*He became a millionaire yesterday.*
Habt ihr das Programm gesehen?	*Did you see the programme?*

C Other useful pronouns are ***man*** (one/you), ***jemand*** (somebody), ***niemand*** (nobody).

Wie schreibt **man** das?	*How do you write that?*
Jemand hat meine Hose gestohlen.	*Somebody has stolen my trousers.*
Niemand hat es gesehen.	*Nobody saw it.*

D There are three words for 'it' (as the subject) in German:

- ***er*** for ***der*** words:
  Er (der Computer) ist ganz neu. — *It (the computer) is brand new.*
- ***sie*** for ***die*** words:
  Sie (die Küche) ist schmutzig. — *It (the kitchen) is dirty.*
- ***es*** for ***das*** words:
  Es (das Hemd) ist zu klein. — *It (the shirt) is too small.*

☆ *These words are quite easy to remember:* ***er*** *is like* ***der, sie*** *like* ***die*** *and* ***es*** *like* ***das****.*

E There are three words for 'you' (as the subject) in German:

– ***du*** is used if you are talking to one friend, one member of your family or one animal.

– ***ihr*** is the plural form of ***du***; use ***ihr*** if you are talking to friends, members of your family or animals.

– ***Sie*** is used if you are talking to one or more older people (teachers, a shop assistant, the bus driver) or people you don't know very well.

F The German word ***sie*** has four meanings (as the subject):

– If it has a capital letter, ***Sie***, it means 'you' (polite).

– If it is written ***sie***, it means 'she', 'it' or 'they'.

G The German word for 'I' is always spelled with a small letter (unless it starts a sentence, of course): ***ich***.

H ***Du/Ihr*** have capital letters when they are written in a letter.

Test your understanding

How would you ask these people what they like reading?

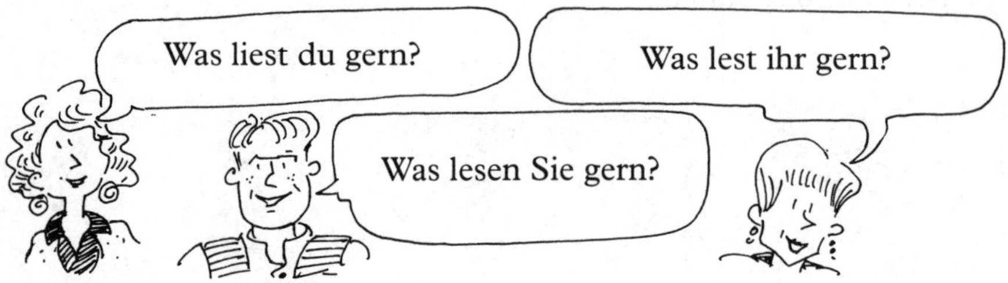

a a 5-year-old boy
b two adult passers-by
c your German teacher
d an 18-year-old cousin
e all the pupils in your class
f your penfriend
g your mum

Rewrite these sentences changing the underlined words for a pronoun.

<u>Die Frau</u> ist ungeduldig. Sie ist ungeduldig.

a <u>Der Hund</u> heißt Hänsi.
b <u>Claudia und ich</u> gehen ins Schwimmbad.
c Wo schlafen <u>die Kinder</u>?
d <u>Das Auto</u> ist kaputt.
e Wo geht <u>Stefan</u> hin?
f Wann geht <u>das Programm</u> zu Ende?

2 *mich, dich, ihn .....*

A Just as the words for ***der***, ***die***, ***das*** change in different cases, so too do some of the pronouns.

B If you are using pronouns as the object of the sentence (⇨ p.12), you need to use the accusative pronouns:

Sie haßt **ihn**. *She hates him.*
Hörst du **uns**? *Can you hear us?*
Er besucht **euch**. *He's visiting you.*

C After the accusative prepositions (***durch***, ***ohne***, ***um***, ***bis***, ***gegen***, ***für***), you need to use the accusative pronouns:

Hast du ein Geschenk für **mich**?	*Have you got a present for me?*
Ich gehe ohne **dich**.	*I'm going without you.*

Note how the pronouns change in English as well: I/me, he/him, we/us.

D This chart shows you how some of the pronouns change in the accusative case:

	I	you	he	she	it	we	you/they	you
Nom	ich	du	er	sie	es	wir	Sie/sie	ihr
Acc	**mich**	**dich**	**ihn**	sie	es	**uns**	Sie/sie	**euch**

Test your understanding

Answer the questions below using accusative pronouns.

Wie findest du den neuen Schüler? Ich finde ihn super.

a	Hast du mein Hemd?	Ja, ich habe ..... hier in der Tasche.
b	Liebt Herr Brinkmann Claudia?	Ja, er liebt .....
c	Hat Stefan diese Socken geklaut?	Nein, er hat ..... gekauft.
d	Sieht der Lehrer Felix und mich?	Nein, er sieht ..... nicht.
e	Was kaufst du für deine Eltern?	Ich kaufe nichts für .....
f	Nimmst du einen Pulli mit?	Nein, ich habe ..... verloren.
g	Lädt Rudi seine Freunde ein?	Ja, er lädt ..... alle am Samstag ein.

Find a short text in a German magazine or book. Replace the nouns with nominative and accusative pronouns. Does the text still make sense?

3 *mir, dir, ihm .....*

A Just as the words for ***der***, ***die***, ***das*** change in the dative case (⇨ p.9), so too do the pronouns.

B If you are talking about people to whom you are doing something, you need to use the dative case for the pronouns.

C After the dative prepositions (***ab***, ***aus***, ***bei***, ***gegenüber***, ***mit***, ***nach***, ***seit***, ***von***, ***zu***), you need to use the dative pronouns. You also have to use them after the dative verbs (⇨ p.13).

Hilft Felix **dir** damit?	*Is Felix helping you with that?*
Der Fahrer folgt **ihm**.	*The driver follows him/it.*
Gabi zeigt **ihr** das Buch.	*Gabi shows her the book.*
Wie geht's **Ihnen**?	*How are you?*

Note how the pronouns change in English as well: (to) me, (to) him, (to) her, (to) us.

D This chart shows you how the pronouns change in the dative case:

	I	you	he	she	it	we	you/they	you
Nom	ich	du	er	sie	es	wir	Sie/sie	ihr
Acc	mich	dich	ihn	sie	es	uns	Sie/sie	euch
Dat	**mir**	**dir**	**ihm**	**ihr**	**ihm**	**uns**	**Ihnen/ihnen**	**euch**

E There are some phrases which always use the dative case pronouns:

Wie geht's Ihnen/dir/euch?	*How are you?*
Mir gefällt Mathe.	*I like Maths.*
Mir ist kalt/warm.	*I'm cold/warm.*
Es tut mir leid.	*I'm sorry.*
Das macht mir Spaß.	*That's fun.*
Das geht mir auf die Nerven.	*That annoys me.*
Was fehlt dir?	*What's the matter?*
Das schmeckt mir nicht.	*I don't like that* (food).
Das Hemd steht mir nicht.	*The shirt doesn't suit me.*
Die Bluse paßt mir nicht.	*The blouse doesn't fit me.*

Test your understanding

Fill in the gaps:

a – Wie findest du meine neue Kassette?
– Sie gefällt ..... gar nicht.

b – Warum bist du immer mit Mehmet?
– Ich gehe mit ..... aus.

c – Was gibst du den Zwillingen zum Geburtstag?
– Ich gebe ..... ein Paar Ohrringe.

d – Hilfst du immer deiner Mutter?
– Leider, ja. Ich muß ..... jeden Nachmittag im Geschäft helfen.

e – Was machst du dauernd bei deiner Freundin?
– Ich spiele Karten mit ..... natürlich.

f – Bring bitte Geschenke für Karl und mich.
– Nein, ich bringe ..... nichts.

g – Willst du mit ..... spielen?
– Was? Mit dir und Franz? Nein, danke!

---

4 Relative pronouns

A Relative pronouns define things and people. They translate 'who/which' when they are not asking a question.

Der Polizist**, der** Pickel hat.	*The policeman who has got spots.*
Die Frau**, die** bei der Bank arbeitet.	*The woman who works at the bank.*
Das Bild**, das** an der Wand hängt.	*The picture which is hanging on the wall.*
Das Buch**, das** auf dem Regal ist.	*The book which is on the shelf.*

Note how there is always a comma before the relative pronoun. Also, there is no difference in German between 'who' and 'which'.

B When you use a relative pronoun, the verb which follows goes to the end of the sentence.

C The relative pronoun always refers back to an item in the first part of the sentence. Its form changes according to its case in the second half of the sentence.

Das ist der Polizist**, der** Pickel hat. *That is the policeman who has spots.*
– ***der*** (masculine nominative) is the relative pronoun here because it is referring to ***der Polizist***, i.e. a masculine noun, and it is in the nominative case, i.e. '**he** has spots'.

Das ist der Polizist**, den** ich mag. *That is the policeman who I like.*
– ***den*** (masculine accusative) is the relative pronoun here because it is referring to ***der Polizist***, i.e. a masculine noun, and it is in the accusative case, i.e. 'I like **him**'.

D The relative pronoun table below is similar to the ***der/die/das*** table (⇨ p.9):

	m	f	n	pl
Nom	der	die	das	die
Acc	den	die	das	die
Dat	dem	der	dem	denen
Gen	dessen	deren	dessen	deren

Das Haus, in **dem** (n/dat) ich wohne, ist groß. — *The house which I live in is big.*

Die Eltern, deren Tochter (pl/gen) taub ist. — *The parents whose daughter is deaf.*

Test your understanding

Look at the picture and name the people.

Das Mädchen, das im Rollstuhl sitzt. Sie heißt Annette.

a Die Frau, die lockige helle Haare hat.
b Der Junge, den man neben der Tür findet.

c Das Kind, das mit dem Ball spielt.
d Der Mann, der in der Telefonzelle ist.
e Der Schüler, dessen Schnürsenkel kaputt ist.
f Die Schülerin, deren Hemd gestreift ist.
g Das Mädchen, das ein Buch liest.

Can you name the following people and things?

a Ein Kind, das keine Geschwister hat.
b Ein Stuhl, der Räder hat.
c Ein Tier, das man zu Hause hat.
d Ein Kind, das weiblich ist.
e Die Institution, in der man Unterricht bekommt.
f Leute, die aus Deutschland kommen.
g Das Zimmer, in dem man sich duscht.

Make up some more definitions for a partner.

Can you describe the people listed below using relative pronouns?

Eine Lehrerin ist eine Frau, die an der Schule unterrichtet.

a ein Arzt
b ein Blinder
c eine Sportlerin
d Jounalistinnen
e ein Friseur
f ein Witwer
g eine Witwe

Summary: Personal pronouns

1 Pronouns are small words which refer to people: ***ich***, ***du***, ***er***.

2 There are three words for 'it' in German: ***er*** (m), ***sie*** (f), ***es*** (n).

3 There are three words for 'you' in German: ***du***, ***Sie***, ***ihr***.

4 ***Sie/sie*** has four meanings: 'she', 'it', 'you', 'they'.

5 Pronouns change in the accusative and dative cases: ***ich***, ***mich***, ***mir ......***

6 Relative pronouns translate 'who/which'.

Hast du's kapiert?

What goes together?

ich – mich – mir

ich	du	er	sie	es	wir	Sie/sie	ihr

dich	ihn	es	uns	sie	euch	Sie/sie	mich

Ihnen/ihnen	mir	ihm	euch	dir	uns	ihr

Rewrite the text below using as many pronouns as possible.

Heute spiele ich Basketball mit meinen Freunden. Meine Freunde und ich spielen einmal in der Woche. Meine Freunde und ich spielen unten im Keller. Es macht meinen Freunden und mir Spaß! Nach dem Spiel gehen meine Freunde zurück in die Stadt. Ich aber nicht. Ich besuche dann meine Freundin. Meine Freundin wohnt in einem Wohnblock. Der Wohnblock ist neben unserem Park. Meine Freundin und ich gehen zusammen ins Eiscafé. Normalerweise ist das Eiscafé sehr romantisch. Leider kommen manchmal Gramma und ihre Freundinnen ins Eiscafé. Gramma und ihre Freundinnen ärgern mich sehr. Gramma und ihre Freundinnen sitzen am Tisch. Dann bestellen Gramma und ihre Freundinnen Eis, und Gramma und ihre Freundinnen kichern. Grisilde und ich verlassen dann das Eiscafé. Grisilde und ich gehen im Park spazieren. Dorthin kommt Gramma nicht, weil sie gegen die Parkbäume allergisch ist.

6 Verbs

- A verb is a doing word. It tells you about actions and feelings. It also tells you about how people and things are, were or are going to be.

Ich **hasse** Mathe.	*I hate Maths.*
Der Hund **hat** meine Hausaufgaben **gegessen.**	*The dog ate my homework.*
Meine Mutter **war** krank.	*My mother was ill.*
Ich **werde** mich gut **benehmen**.	*I will behave myself.*

- If you look up a verb in the dictionary, you will find its infinitive form. Most German infinitives end in **-en** (a few end in just **-n**): lauf**en** (to run), geh**en** (to go), hab**en** (to have), sei**n** (to be).

- A verb always has to match its subject (the person doing the action of the verb), and it changes accordingly. This happens in English as well:

  ärgern (to annoy)
  ich ärger**e**/er ärger**t** (I annoy/he annoy**s**)

- Actions happen at different times. Different tenses describe these times:
  - the present tense (⇨ p.51) tells you about what is happening now;
  - the perfect tense (⇨ p.60) tells you about things which have already happened;
  - the simple past (⇨ p.68) describes things which were happening earlier or used to happen;
  - the pluperfect tense (⇨ p.78) describes things which had happened;
  - the future tense (⇨ p.76) describes things which are going to happen.

Grammar in action

Find the verbs in this text and write them in their infinitive form. What do they mean in English?

4X4 Off Road (Amiga)
Der Spieler fährt mit dem Truck. Andere Wagen sind auch auf dem Gelände. Der Spieler überholt diese Wagen. Dabei gewinnt er Punkte. Zur gleichen Zeit kommen Hindernisse. Der Spieler versucht, diese Hindernissen zu vermeiden.

1 The present tense

A When you learn the present tense in German, you learn three tenses in one! The present tense in German can have three meanings:

ich weine can mean:
– I cry
– I am crying
– I am going to cry.

2 Regular verbs (present tense)

A Remember that verbs have to match their subject. Many German verbs follow the same pattern in the present tense to do this. These verbs are called regular verbs.

B For the present tense of regular verbs, you take off the ***-en/n*** of the infinitive and add these endings:

spielen (to play)
ich spiel**e**
du spiel**st**
er/sie/es spiel**t**
wir/sie/Sie spiel**en**
ihr spiel**t**

☆ *Try and learn this pattern. The* ***wir/sie/Sie*** *form is always the same as the infinitive and the* ***er*** *and* ***ihr*** *ending is the same, so you've only got four endings to learn!*

Test your understanding

Write these verbs in their different forms. They are all regular in the present tense.

lachen (to laugh)
ich lache
du lachst
er/sie/es lacht
wir/sie/Sie lachen
ihr lacht

a hören
b machen
c sagen
d rennen
e studieren
f rufen
g klettern

Complete the sentences below with the correct form of the verb in the present tense.

a Was ..... du hinter der Tür?
b Carola ..... sehr laut Elektrogitarre.
c ..... ihr gern diese schreckliche Musik?

d Heidi und Saskia ..... auf den Tisch.
e Den ganzen Sommer ..... wir im Gartenteich.
f Wo ..... Sie?
g Ich ..... dich!

machen	**spielen**	**hören**	**springen**
wohnen	**lieben**	**angeln**	

---

3 Irregular verbs (present tense)

A Not all German verbs follow the same pattern for the present tense. These verbs are called irregular verbs.

B Irregular verbs have the same endings as the regular verbs (⇨ p.52) but there is also a change in the ***du*** and ***er/sie/es*** forms. (***ich***, ***wir***, ***sie***, ***Sie***, ***ihr*** are like the regular verbs.)

essen (to eat)
ich esse
du **i**ßt
er/sie/es **i**ßt
wir/sie/Sie essen
ihr eßt

– Sometimes, the first **e** changes to ***i(e)***:

essen (to eat)	ich esse	du **i**ßt	er/sie/es **i**ßt
geben (to give)	ich gebe	du g**i**bst	er/sie/es g**i**bt
nehmen (to take)	ich nehme	du n**i**mmst	er/sie/es n**i**mmt
sprechen (to speak)	ich spreche	du spr**i**chst	er/sie/es spr**i**cht
lesen (to read)	ich lese	du l**ie**st	er/sie/es l**ie**st
sehen (to see)	ich sehe	du s**ie**hst	er/sie/es s**ie**ht

– Sometimes, ***a*** becomes ***ä***:

fahren (to drive)	ich fahre	du f**ä**hrst	er/sie/es f**ä**hrt
fallen (to fall)	ich falle	du f**ä**llst	er/sie/es f**ä**llt
fangen (to catch)	ich fange	du f**ä**ngst	er/sie/es f**ä**ngt
halten (to stop)	ich halte	du h**ä**ltst	er/sie/es h**ä**lt
lassen (to leave)	ich lasse	du l**ä**ßt	er/sie/es l**ä**ßt
laufen (to run)	ich laufe	du l**ä**ufst	er/sie/es l**ä**uft
tragen (to carry; wear)	ich trage	du tr**ä**gst	er/sie/es tr**ä**gt

– For verbs ending in ***-den*** or ***-ten***, you keep the **e** of the infinitive so you can say the verbs!

arbeiten (to work)	ich arbeite	du arbeit**e**st	er/sie/es arbeit**e**t
finden (to find)	ich finde	du find**e**st	er/sie/es find**e**t

– For verbs ending in ***-sen***, ***-ßen***, ***-ssen***, ***-zen***, the ***du*** form is like the ***er/sie/es*** form:

niesen (to sneeze)	ich niese	du/er/sie/es niest
heißen (to be called)	ich heiße	du/er/sie/es heißt
hassen (to hate)	ich hasse	du/er/sie/es haßt
tanzen (to dance)	ich tanze	du/er/sie/es tanzt

Test your understanding

Choose the correct form of the verb:

a Wo finde/findest ich die Toilette, bitte?
b Was ißt/esse er zum Frühstück?
c Sprichst/sprechen Sie Deutsch?
d Du fährst/fährt hier links und dann immer geradeaus.
e Sehen/seht ihr das Schild nicht?
f Ich nehme/nehmen eine Tasse Tee, bitte.
g Hier gibt/gibst es keine freien Zimmer.

Complete this report filling in the appropriate forms of the verbs in brackets.

Ich ..... (sehen) eine Frau im Geschäft. Sie ..... (sprechen) mit einem Mann. Der Mann ..... (arbeiten) in der Kinderabteilung. Jetzt ..... (gehen) sie zur Kasse. Die Frau ..... (nehmen) etwas aus der Tasche. Der Mann ..... (geben) ihr etwas aus der Kasse. Dann ..... (fallen) er plötzlich hin. Die Frau ..... (laufen) aus dem Geschäft. Dort ..... (stehen) ein roter Mercedes. Die Frau ..... (steigen) in das Auto. Sie ..... (fahren) weg. Wir ..... (folgen) schnell hinterher.

4 *haben and sein*

A You use the verbs ***haben*** (to have) and ***sein*** (to be) a lot in German so it's worth learning them off by heart at an early stage.

B This is how they go in the present tense:

haben (to have)
ich habe
du hast
er/sie/es hat
wir/sie/Sie haben
ihr habt

sein (to be)
ich bin
du bist
er/sie/es ist
wir/sie/Sie sind
ihr seid

C Note how ***haben*** is used in these phrases:

Ich habe Durst.	*I'm thirsty.*
Ich habe Hunger.	*I'm hungry.*
Ich habe (keine) Lust.	*I (don't) want to.*
Ich habe Angst.	*I'm afraid.*

Test your understanding

Translate these sentences into German.

a I'm in a bad mood.
b They are very nice.
c I've got a headache.
d We've got a new computer.
e Have you (to a child) got your jacket?
f She hasn't got any friends.
g You (to two children) are very cheeky.

Kopfschmerzen **keine Freunde** **schlecht gelaunt**
sehr frech **sehr sympathisch**
einen neuen Computer **deine Jacke**

5 Commands

A If you want to tell someone or several people to do something, you use a command.

B Commands are always in the present tense. Their form varies, depending on whom you are speaking to.

C If you are addressing someone as ***Sie*** (⇨ p.41) you use the infinitive of the verb and put it at the start of the sentence:

Gehen Sie hier rechts!	*Go right here.*
Kaufen Sie hier nicht ein!	*Don't do your shopping here.*
Passen Sie bitte auf!	*Please be careful.*

D If you are addressing people as ***ihr*** (⇨ p.41) you use the present tense ***ihr*** form of the verb and leave out the word ***ihr***:

Macht das Buch zu!	*Close your book.*
Steht bitte auf!	*Stand up please.*
Arbeitet zu dritt.	*Work in threes.*

E If you are addressing someone as ***du*** (⇨ p.41) you use the present tense ***er/sie/es*** form of the verb without the final ***t***:

Sing mit mir!	*Sing with me.*
Nenn eine Stadt in Deutschland!	*Name a town in Germany.*
Lach nicht so laut!	*Don't laugh so loud.*

If an *umlaut* has been added in the present tense, leave it off for the command: ***er/sie/es schläft*** – ***schlaf gut!***

F The exception to the above rule is the verb ***sein*** (to be):

(du)	**Sei** bitte ruhig!	*Please be quiet.*
(Sie)	**Seien Sie** bitte ruhig!	*Please be quiet.*
(ihr)	**Seid** bitte ruhig!	*Please be quiet.*

Test your understanding

Tell these people what to do!

Sie – Schokolade kaufen   Kaufen Sie Schokolade!

a du – einen Kopfstand machen
b ihr – ein schönes Bild zeichnen
c du – ein Lied singen
d Sie – auf einem Bein stehen
e du – nicht so frech sein
f Sie – bis hundert zählen
g ihr – eure Partner kitzeln

6 Reflexive verbs

A Some verbs need to be used with a reflexive pronoun (myself, yourself, ...).

sich rasieren (to shave)
ich rasiere **mich**
du rasierst **dich**
er/sie/es rasiert **sich**
wir rasieren **uns**
sie/Sie rasieren **sich**
ihr rasiert **euch**

B Here are some reflexive verbs:

sich erinnern an	(to remember)
sich interessieren (für)	(to be interested [in])
sich langweilen	(to be bored)
sich anziehen	(to get dressed)
sich umziehen	(to change)
sich ausziehen	(to get undressed)
sich duschen	(to shower)
sich waschen	(to wash yourself)
sich umsehen	(to look around)

C The reflexive pronoun (***mich***, ***dich***, ***sich*** .....) comes after the main verb in a sentence.

Ich wasche **mich**.	*I wash myself.*
Sie interessieren **sich** für Geschichte.	*They are interested in history.*

D The reflexive pronoun (***mich***, ***dich***, ***sich*** .....) comes after the subject in a question.

Ziehen wir **uns** um?	*Shall we get changed?*
Erinnert Dirk **sich** an das Mädchen?	*Does Dirk remember the girl?*

Test your understanding

Fill in the correct reflexive pronoun in each of the following sentences.

a Er zieht ..... an.
b Wir interessieren ..... gar nicht für Musik.
c Wie habt ihr ..... daran erinnert?

d Wie oft waschen Sie ..... am Tag?
e Wie ziehst du ..... an?
f Ich sehe ..... in der Stadt gern um.
g Sie langweilt .....!

Mime an action of a reflexive verb to a partner. Can your partner say what you are doing?

Du rasierst dich.

Summary: Verbs in the present tense

1 Verbs are words of action which tell you what someone or something is doing or feeling.

2 The infinitive form of German verbs ends in ***-en*** or ***-n***.

3 You have to add endings to verbs to match the person doing the action: ***fühlen/ich fühle/du fühlst***.

4 Regular verbs follow the same pattern.

5 Irregular verbs have a change in the middle of the word, but they take the same endings as the regular verbs.

6 Two important verbs which need to be learned separately are ***haben*** (to have) and ***sein*** (to be).

7 You use the present tense forms to make commands.

8 Some verbs need a reflexive pronoun to complete their meaning.

9 The list on page 73 shows some useful irregular verbs in the present tense.

Hast du's kapiert?

Answer these questions.

a Wo wohnst du?
b Was für Bücher liest du gern?
c Was trägst du zur Schule?
d Was ißt du zum Frühstück?
e Woher kommst du?
f Wie heißt deine Lieblingsgruppe?
g Was machst du am Wochenende?

Complete this report filling in the appropriate forms of the verbs in brackets.

Wir ..... (folgen) dem Mercedes die Straße entlang. Er ..... (haben) das Kennzeichen M. Sicher ..... (kommen) das Auto aus München. Die Frau ..... (sein) ziemlich klein. Sie ..... (haben) blaue Haare und ..... (tragen) eine gelbe Jacke und einen Hut mit Blumen drauf. Bald ..... (erreichen) wir die Autobahn. Die Frau ..... (fahren) auf die Autobahn in Richtung Süden. Es ..... (sein) sehr dunkel auf der Autobahn, und es ..... (regnen) stark. Plötzlich ..... (halten) die Frau auf der rechten Fahrbahn. Sie ..... (steigen) aus dem Auto.
»Was ..... (machen) Sie dort?« ..... (rufen) ich aus dem Fenster. ».... (sein) Sie verrückt?«
»Nein«, ... (antworten) sie, »ich ..... (sein) Gräfin Gramm, und ich ..... (haben) kein Benzin mehr. ..... (nehmen) Sie mich bitte mit zum Schloß?«

Look at the picture below. How many action words can you think of to describe it?

Zwei Leute **spielen** Badminton.

7 The perfect tense

- The perfect tense is used for talking about things which have happened before now, i.e. in the past:

Am Montag **hat** Fritz das Abendessen **gemacht**.	*Fritz cooked tea on Monday.*
Am Dienstag **habe** ich Magenschmerzen **gehabt**.	*On Tuesday I had stomach ache.*
Am Mittwoch **bin** ich zur Ärztin **gegangen**.	*On Wednesday I went to the doctor.*
Gestern **habe** ich zu Hause **gegessen**.	*Yesterday I ate at home.*

- In German, the perfect tense has three parts:
  - person/subject (***ich***, ***Erwin***, ***Emine*** .....)
  - the present tense of ***haben*** or ***sein*** (⇨ p.55)
  - the verb in its perfect tense form (past participle).

- Past participles are easy to spot because they nearly always start with **ge-** and end with ***-t*** or ***-en***:

gegessen	(eaten)
geklatscht	(clapped)
gehört	(heard)

- Each verb has one past participle form. It is the form of ***haben*** or ***sein*** which must match the subject of the sentence:

Am Montag **habe** ich den Wecker nicht **gehört**.	*I didn't hear the alarm clock on Monday.*
Gestern **hat** Oliver den Wecker nicht **gehört**.	*Oliver didn't hear the alarm yesterday.*
Wir **sind** nach Istanbul **gegangen**.	*We walked to Istanbul.*
Hannah **ist** zum Kino **gegangen**.	*Hannah walked to the cinema.*

- Look at the position of the words in bold type above. ***haben*** or ***sein*** goes where the main verb normally goes (⇨ p.94) and the past participle goes to the end of the sentence.

Grammar in action
How many examples of the perfect tense can you find in this notice?
What do they mean in English?

Ich habe meine kleine Katze verloren. Sie heißt Mitzi und ist zwei Jahre alt. Sie wohnt in der Fridolinstr. 22. Haben Sie sie gesehen? Sie ist schwarz und weiß.

1 Regular verbs (perfect tense)

A Most regular verbs form their past participle by:

- adding **ge-** to the start of the infinitive
- changing the final ***-en/n*** to ***-t***.

hören (to hear)	**ge**hör**t** (heard)
machen (to do)	**ge**mach**t** (done)
sagen (to say)	**ge**sag**t** (said)
klettern (to climb)	**ge**kletter**t** (climbed)

B All regular verbs use ***haben*** for the perfect tense:

Gabi **hat** ein Buch gekauft.	*Gabi bought a book.*
Du **hast** nichts gemacht.	*You didn't do anything.*
Was **haben** sie gesagt?	*What did they say?*

C You don't have to add **ge-** to verbs beginning with **be-**, ***ent-***, ***er-***, **ge-**, ***ver-***, ***zer-*** , or ending in ***-ieren***:

bestellen (to order)	bestellt
entdecken (to discover)	entdeckt
erzählen (to tell)	erzählt
verdienen (to earn)	verdient
trainieren (to train)	trainiert

D Separable verbs (⇨ p.101) put the **ge** in the middle:

auf/räumen (to tidy up)	auf**ge**räumt
um/tauschen (to swap)	um**ge**tauscht
staub/saugen (to vacuum)	staub**ge**saugt

Test your understanding ▼▼▼

Write the infinitives of these past participles with their English meaning.

gesagt (said) – sagen (to say)

a gestellt
b gelacht
c gekauft
d geklatscht
e geplaudert
f aufgepaßt
g telefoniert

Write these sentences in the perfect tense.

Beethoven hört nichts. – Beethoven hat nichts gehört.

a Mozart wohnt in Salzburg.
b Beckenbauer spielt Fußball.
c Einstein entdeckt die Relativitätstheorie.
d Die Brüder Grimm erzählen viele Märchen.
e Gustav Klimt malt Bilder.
f Marlene Dietrich spielt oft Theater.
g Karl Benz stellt das erste Auto her.

▲▲

2 Irregular verbs (perfect tense)

A Irregular verbs form their past participle by:

- adding **ge-** to the start of the infinitive
- sometimes changing their letters in the middle.

fahren/**ge**fahren singen/**ge**s**u**ngen gehen/**ge**ga**ng**en

B Most irregular verbs use ***haben*** for the perfect tense, but some use ***sein*** (⇨ p.65):

Du **bist** zu schnell **gefahren**.	*You drove too fast.*
Das Boot **ist gesunken**.	*The boat sank.*

c The lists below show you the past participles of some irregular verbs. The ones marked * take ***sein***.

– These irregular verbs simply add **ge-** to the infinitive:

essen (to eat)	gegessen
fahren (to drive)	gefahren*
fallen (to fall)	gefallen*
fangen (to catch)	gefangen
geben (to give)	gegeben
kommen (to come)	gekommen*
lassen (to leave)	gelassen
laufen (to run)	gelaufen*
lesen (to read)	gelesen
rufen (to call)	gerufen
schlafen (to sleep)	geschlafen
schlagen (to hit)	geschlagen
sehen (to see)	gesehen
tragen (to carry; wear)	getragen
waschen (to wash)	gewaschen

– These irregular verbs change the ***ei*** to ***ie***:

bleiben (to stay)	geblieben*
schreiben (to write)	geschrieben
steigen (to climb)	gestiegen*
leihen (to lend)	geliehen
treiben (to do, make)	getrieben

– These irregular verbs have **o** in their past participle:

bieten (to offer)	geboten
beginnen (to begin)	begonnen
brechen (to break)	gebrochen
fliegen (to fly)	geflogen*
gewinnen (to win)	gewonnen
helfen (to help)	geholfen
nehmen (to take)	genommen
schließen (to shut)	geschlossen
schwimmen (to swim)	geschwommen*
sprechen (to speak)	gesprochen
sterben (to die)	gestorben*
treffen (to hit; meet)	getroffen
verlieren (to lose)	verloren
werfen (to throw)	geworfen
ziehen (to pull)	gezogen

– These irregular verbs have ***u*** in their past participle:

finden (to find)	gefunden
singen (to sing)	gesungen
sinken (to sink)	gesunken*
springen (to jump)	gesprungen*
stinken (to stink)	gestunken
trinken (to drink)	getrunken
zwingen (to force)	gezwungen

– These are irregular past participles too:

gehen (to go)	gegangen*
liegen (to lie)	gelegen
sein (to be)	gewesen*
stehen (to stand)	gestanden*
tun (to do)	getan
werden (to become)	geworden*
bringen (to bring)	gebracht
denken (to think)	gedacht
kennen (to know)	gekannt
wissen (to know)	gewußt

☆ *Make some verb cards to help you learn these past participles. Cut up a sheet of card into small pieces. Write an infinitive on one side of each piece and its past participle on the other. You can now test yourself by looking at the infinitive and saying the past participle. Turn over the card to see if you are right!*

D Some of the verbs marked with * can also take ***haben*** in the perfect tense. They do this when there is a direct object in the sentence:

Meine Mutter **hat** das Auto **gefahren**.	*My mother drove the car.*
Sie **ist** in die Stadt **gefahren**.	*She drove to town.*

Test your understanding

Write the rhymes out using the correct pair of matching past participles from the box.

a Ich habe nichts .....
Du hast aber nicht .....

b Wann bist du hier .....?
Und was hast du von hier .....?

c Was haben Sie gestern .....?
Ihr Zimmer hat wohl .....!

d Habt ihr Sport .....?
Ich bin zu Hause .....

e Sie hat das Buch .....
Dann ist sie traurig .....

f Er hat mit mir .....
Dann hat er meinen Teller .....

g Wir haben ein Lied .....
Dann ist die Katze aus dem Fenster .....!

gelesen	**gesprochen**	**gesungen**	**geblieben**
gekommen	**gestunken**	**gebrochen**	**gemacht**
genommen	**getrieben**	**gesprungen**	**getrunken**
	gewesen	**gedacht**	

Can you make up more rhymes using past participles?

Write the past participles and the English meaning of the following verbs.

singen (to sing) – gesungen (sung)

a geben
b gehen
c beginnen
d treiben
e trinken
f denken
g schlafen

3 *haben* or *sein* in the perfect tense

A All regular verbs use ***haben*** in the perfect tense.

Gestern **hat** Sabine eine Torte gemacht. *Sabine made a cake yesterday.*
Wir **haben** dir ein Geschenk gekauft. *We bought you a present.*
Du **hast** Fußball gespielt. *You played football.*

B Many irregular verbs use ***sein*** in the perfect tense. These verbs are often verbs to do with movement from one place to another.

Ich **bin** nach Hause **gekommen**. *I came home.*
Wir **sind** nach Spanien **gefahren**. *We went to Spain.*
Er **ist** beim Klettern **gefallen**. *He fell while climbing.*

3 These are some common verbs which take ***sein*** in the perfect tense:

bleiben, gehen, fahren, fallen, fliegen, kommen, laufen, schwimmen, sein, sinken, springen, steigen, sterben, werden.

Test your understanding

Say what happened in the following years. (Remember that some verbs take ***sein***!)

1939 – der Zweite Weltkrieg beginnt! – 1939 hat der Zweite Weltkrieg begonnen.

a 1989 – die Mauer fällt!
b 1969 – ein Mann fliegt zum Mond!
c 1990 – Deutschland gewinnt die Fußballweltmeisterschaft!
d 1960 – Frauen in der Schweiz bekommen das Wahlrecht!
e 1916 – Franz Josef stirbt!
f 1865 – Wagner schreibt *Tristan und Isolde!*
g 1945 – der Zweite Weltkrieg geht zu Ende!

Summary: Verbs in the perfect tense

1 The perfect tense describes things which have already happened.

2 The perfect tense has three parts: a person/subject, ***haben/sein*** and a past participle.

3 ***haben*** or ***sein*** go where the main verb goes in a sentence and the past participle goes to the end of the sentence.

4 Regular verbs form their past participle by adding **ge-** to the beginning of the infinitive and changing the ***-en*** at the end to ***-t***.

5 Irregular verbs form their past participle by adding **ge-** to the beginning of the infinitive and changing some letters in the middle. These need to be learned separately.

6 Most verbs use ***haben*** in the perfect tense.

7 Verbs which show movement towards somewhere use ***sein*** in the perfect tense.

8 The list on page 73 shows some useful irregular verbs in the perfect tense.

Hast du's kapiert?

Describe what Gramma did on Saturday.

Am Samstagvormittag hat Gramma die Schildkröte gewaschen.

Answer the following questions.

a Was hast du gestern zum Abendessen gegessen?
b Wann bist du vorgestern ins Bett gegangen?
c Was hast du zu deinem zehnten Geburtstag bekommen?
d Wo bist du geboren?
e Wie oft bist du letztes Jahr ins Kino gegangen?
f Welche Stunden hast du letzten Mittwoch gehabt?
g Was hast du letztes Wochenende gemacht?

8 *The simple past*

- The simple past is mainly used when you write about things which have already happened. Most stories about earlier events are written in the simple past.
- The simple past translates the English 'was/were doing' something:

Ich **ging** die Straße entlang.	*I was going along the street.*
Ein Vogel **flog** über mir.	*A bird was flying above me.*

- The simple past also translates 'used to do' something:

Als Teenager **liebte** ich Popmusik.	*As a teenager I used to love pop music.*
Meine Eltern **blieben** in der Küche.	*My parents used to stay in the kitchen.*

Grammar in action

Translate this article into English.

Eine Meile. Vier Minuten.

AM 6. Mai 1954 war es kühl und windig. Viele Leute trafen sich auf dem Iffley Road Track in Oxford. Unter ihnen war der junge englische Medizinstudent Roger Bannister. Er trug weiße Shorts und ein weißes T-Shirt. Sein Ziel war es, eine Meile in vier Minuten zu schaffen. Sein Ziel erreichte er in drei Minuten und 59,4 Sekunden. Es gab einen neuen Weltrekord.

1 Regular verbs

A Regular verbs all follow a pattern in the simple past. Take off the ***-en/ -n*** of the infinitive and add these endings:

spielen (to play)
ich spiel**te**
du spiel**test**
er/sie/es spiel**te**
wir/sie/Sie spiel**ten**
ihr spiel**tet**

☆ *This pattern is very similar to the present tense pattern (⇨ p.52) but all the forms need an extra **t**.*

B For verbs ending in ***-den*** or ***-ten***, you keep the **e** of the infinitive so you can say the verbs!

arbeiten   ich arbeit**e**te   du arbeit**e**test   er arbeit**e**te

Test your understanding
Rewrite this story in the simple past.

Am Samstagvormittag spielte ich Tennis .....

Am Samstagvormittag spiele ich Tennis mit meinem Bruder. Es regnet, aber das macht uns nichts aus. Nach einer Weile hören wir ein Geräusch. Wir schauen uns um und beobachten eine kleine Katze hoch in einem Baum. Die Katze weint. Mein Bruder lacht laut, aber ich lache nicht. Ich versuche, der Katze zu helfen, aber ich erreiche sie nicht. Mein Bruder sucht seinen alten Tennisschläger. Er klettert den Baum hinauf und erreicht die Katze mit dem Schläger. Die Katze kratzt meinen Bruder am Arm. Mein Bruder lächelt nicht.

2 Irregular verbs

A There are some irregular verbs which are often used in the simple past:

sein (to be)   war (was)
haben (to have)   hatte (had)
es gibt (there is/are)   es gab (there was/were)

dürfen (to be allowed to)   durfte (was allowed to)
können (to be able to)   konnte (could)
müssen (to have to)   mußte (had to)
sollen (ought to)   sollte (should)
wollen (to want to)   wollte (wanted to)

Ich **war** müde.	*I was tired.*
Atabak **hatte** Kopfschmerzen.	*Atabak had a headache.*
Wir **wollten** das nicht machen.	*We didn't want to do that.*

B Irregular verbs follow a pattern for their endings in the simple past. They change part of the infinitive first though. These changes need to be learned separately. The list on page 73 shows you the irregular verb forms for the simple past.

C Once you have found the irregular form of the verb, you add these endings to it:

geben (to give)
ich gab
du gab**st**
er/sie/es gab
wir/sie/Sie gab**en**
ihr gab**t**

Test your understanding

Find the infinitives for these simple past forms. You can use the list on page 73 to help you.

flog – fliegen (to fly)

a gewann
b lag
c nahm
d ließ
e sang
f sprach
g verlor

Write these sentences in the simple past.

Früher ..... man keine Elektrizität. (haben)
Früher hatte man keine Elektrizität.

a In den sechziger Jahren ..... man Miniröcke. (tragen)
b Dinosaurier ..... auf unserer Erde. (leben)
c In den fünfziger Jahren ..... Frauen nicht so viel wie heutzutage. (arbeiten)
d Im letzten Jahrhundert ..... es keine Autos. (geben)

e Vor einigen Jahren ..... man Rostock ohne Visum nicht besuchen. (können)
f In der Vergangenheit ..... alles oft besser zu sein. (scheinen)
g Vor der Vereinigung ..... Deutschland ein geteiltes Land. (sein)

Can you write some more sentences to explain how things used to be?

Summary: Verbs in the simple past

1. The simple past is used in written accounts of things which have already happened.
2. The simple past translates the English 'was/were doing' something or 'used to do' something.
3. Regular verbs follow a pattern in the simple past. You take the **-en/-n** off the infinitive and add endings.
4. Irregular verbs follow a pattern for their endings but the main part of the verb needs to be learned separately.
5. The list on page 73 shows some useful irregular verbs in the simple past.

Hast du's kapiert?

Oma Gramm is telling Grimmi about Graf Gramm when he was young. Fill in the verbs taken from the box on the next page.

Ach, dein Vater ..... ein schreckliches Kind. Jeden Tag ..... er brav ins Kindergarten. Jeden Tag ..... der Lehrer ihn wieder nach Hause. In der Klasse ..... er immer Dummheiten. Entweder ..... er Spinnen ins Butterbrot der anderen Kinder, oder ..... er laut, als der Lehrer was sagen ..... Eines Tages ..... er mit einem Brief nach Hause. Der Lehrer ..... die Nase voll von ihm. Er ..... nicht wieder zur Klasse gehen. Natürlich ..... er das wunderbar. Ich aber nicht. Ich ..... ihn zu Hause unterrichten.

sein	gehen	schicken	machen
stecken	singen	wollen	kommen
haben	können	finden	müssen

What were you like when you were very young? Write sentences to describe yourself.

9 Verb list

- If you are not sure how irregular verbs form their present, perfect or simple past tense, you can always look them up in a list like the one below. Most dictionaries give you a list of verbs as well.

- The list below is a selection of some useful verbs you should try and learn. The list shows you:
  - the infinitive form (to do something)
  - the present tense of irregular verbs (remember, it is only the ***er/sie/es*** and ***du*** forms which are irregular)
  - the simple past form (remember these need endings as well, ⇨ p.70)
  - the past participle (remember, verbs marked * take ***sein***)
  - the English meaning.

Infinitive	Present (er/sie/es, du)	Simple past	Past participle	English
beginnen		begann	begonnen	*to begin*
bieten	bietet/bietest	bot	geboten	*to ask*
bitten	bittet/bittest	bat	gebeten	*to request*
bleiben		blieb	geblieben *	*to stay*
brechen	bricht/brichst	brach	gebrochen	*to break*
bringen		brachte	gebracht	*to bring*
denken		dachte	gedacht	*to think*
dürfen	darf/darfst	durfte		*to be allowed to*
einladen	lädt/lädst ein	lud ein	eingeladen	*to invite*
essen	ißt/ißt	aß	gegessen	*to eat*
fahren	fährt/fährst	fuhr	gefahren *	*to drive*
fallen	fällt/fällst	fiel	gefallen *	*to fall*
fangen	fängt/fängst	fing	gefangen	*to catch*

finden	findet/findest	fand	gefunden	*to find*
fliegen		flog	geflogen *	*to fly*
geben	gibt/gibst	gab	gegeben	*to give*
gehen		ging	gegangen	*to walk, go*
gelingen		gelang	gelungen *	*to succeed, reach*
gewinnen		gewann	gewonnen	*to win*
haben	hat/hast	hatte	gehabt	*to have*
halten	hält/hältst	hielt	gehalten	*to stop*
heben		hob	gehoben	*to lift*
heißen	heißt/heißt	hieß	geheißen	*to be called*
helfen	hilft/hilfst	half	geholfen	*to help*
kennen		kannte	gekannt	*to know*
kommen		kam	gekommen *	*to come*
können	kann/kannst	konnte		*to be able to*
lassen	läßt/läßt	ließ	gelassen	*to leave*
laufen	läuft/läufst	lief	gelaufen *	*to run*
lesen	liest/liest	las	gelesen	*to read*
liegen		lag	gelegen	*to lie*
mögen	mag/magst	mochte	gemocht	*to like (to)*
müssen	muß/mußt	mußte		*to have to*
nehmen	nimmt/nimmst	nahm	genommen	*to take*
rufen		rief	gerufen	*to call*
schlafen	schläft/schläfst	schlief	geschlafen	*to sleep*
schlagen	schlägt/schlägst	schlug	geschlagen	*to hit*
schließen	schließt/schließt	schloß	geschlossen	*to close*
schneiden		schnitt	geschnitten	*to cut*
schreiben		schrieb	geschrieben	*to write*
schwimmen		schwamm	geschwommen *	*to swim*

sehen	sieht/siehst	sah	gesehen	*to see*
sein	ist/bist	war	gewesen *	*to be*
singen		sang	gesungen	*to sing*
sitzen	sitzt/sitzt	saß	gesessen	*to sit*
sollen	soll/sollst	sollte		*should*
sprechen	spricht/sprichst	sprach	gesprochen	*to speak*
stehen		stand	gestanden *	*to stand*
steigen		stieg	gestiegen *	*to climb*
stinken		stank	gestunken	*to stink*
tragen	trägt/trägst	trug	getragen	*to wear, carry*
treffen	trifft/triffst	traf	getroffen	*to meet*
trinken		trank	getrunken	*to drink*
tun	tut/tust	tat	getan	*to do*
vergessen	vergißt/vergißt	vergaß	vergessen	*to forget*
verlieren		verlor	verloren	*to lose*
waschen	wäscht/wäscht	wusch	gewaschen	*to wash*
werden	wird/wirst	wurde	geworden *	*to become*
werfen	wirft/wirfst	warf	geworfen	*to throw*
wissen	weiß/weißt	wußte	gewußt	*to know*
wollen	will/willst	wollte		*to want to*
ziehen		zog	gezogen	*to pull*

10 Other tenses

1 The future tense

A The future tense is used to talk about things which are going to or will happen.

B If you want to talk about future events in German, you can use either the present tense (⇨ p.51) or the future tense.

C Most of the time you can use the present tense and other words in the sentence will show that you are talking about future events. This is also the case in English.

Nächste Woche **gibt** es keine Schule.	*There's no school next week.*
Am Montag **bleibe** ich im Bett.	*I'm staying in bed on Monday.*
Kommst du am Dienstag zu mir?	*Are you coming to my house on Tuesday?*

D Use the future tense to make it absolutely clear that you are talking about actions that will or are going to happen.

E To form the future tense you need an infinitive and a part of **werden** (to become):

werden
ich werde
du wirst
er/sie/es wird
wir/sie/Sie werden
ihr werdet

F In the future tense, **werden** works like the main verb in the sentence (i.e. it comes as the second idea) and the infinitive goes to the end of the sentence.

Wir **werden** eine Katastrophe **erleben**.	*We'll experience a catastrophe.*
Hunde **werden** Computerspiele **spielen**.	*Dogs will play computer games.*
Im Jahre 2070 **wirst** du unter Wasser **wohnen**.	*In 2070 you'll live under water.*
Wird es noch Autos auf der Straße **geben**?	*Will there still be cars on the road?*

G The following expressions are useful when you are talking about future events:

morgen	(tomorrow)
übermorgen	(the day after tomorrow)
heute morgen	(this morning)
heute nachmittag	(this afternoon)
heute abend	(this evening)
nächste Woche	(next week)
nächsten Monat	(next month)
nächstes Jahr	(next year)

Test your understanding

Write these sentences in the future tense.

Heute ist es kalt (morgen/warm sein) – Heute ist es kalt, aber morgen wird es warm sein.

a Heute bin ich krank (nächste Woche/wieder fit sein)
b Dieses Jahr macht Gerd das Abitur (nächstes Jahr/auf die Uni gehen)
c Morgen habe ich Geburtstag (am Wochenende/eine Party haben)
d Das letzte Spiel haben wir verloren (das nächste Spiel/gewinnen)
e Heute hast du viele Stunden (heute abend/viele Hausaufgaben haben)
f Heute spielt sie Schach (nächste Woche/Karten spielen)
g Jetzt fahren wir mit dem Auto (im nächsten Jahrhundert/mit dem Elektromofa fahren)

What are your plans for the future? Write a few sentences about them. The words below might help you.

Nächsten Montag	**Nächstes Wochenende .....**
In den nächsten Ferien	**Nächstes Jahr .....**
Nach der Schule	**Im Jahre 2040 .....**

Can you talk about your family's and friends' plans as well?

2 The pluperfect tense

A The pluperfect tense translates the English 'had' done something:

Er **hatte** nichts **gegessen**. *He hadn't eaten anything.*
Ich **war** krank **gewesen**. *I had been ill.*

B The pluperfect is formed by using the past participle (⇨ pp.60–64) with the simple past form of ***haben/sein***:

Wir **hatten** Angst **gehabt**.	*We had been afraid.*
Ich **hatte** nur Bahnhof **verstanden**.	*I hadn't understood a thing.*
Er **war** aus dem Baum **gefallen**.	*He had fallen out of the tree.*
War sie alleine **gewesen**?	*Had she been on her own?*

☆ *The pluperfect works in a very similar way to the perfect tense.*

C The simple past forms of ***haben*** and ***sein*** are given below:

haben (to have)
ich hatte
du hattest
er/sie/es hatte
wir/sie/Sie hatten
ihr hattet

sein (to be)
ich war
du warst
er/sie/es war
wir/sie/Sie waren
ihr wart

Test your understanding

Nobody turned up for football practice on Saturday morning. What were the excuses?

Uli/den Wecker nicht hören – Uli hatte den Wecker nicht gehört.

a Florian/den Bus verpassen
b Thomas und Xavier/einen Unfall haben
c Mehmet/krank sein
d Joachim/zum Arzt gehen
e Nina/Kopfschmerzen haben
f Kai und sein Bruder/ihre Sportsachen verlieren
g Lisa und Markus/einkaufen gehen

Summary: Other tenses

1. You can use the present tense or the future tense to talk about things which are going to happen.
2. For the future tense you need the verb **werden** (to become) and an infinitive.
3. There are some expressions of time which are useful for talking about the future.
4. The pluperfect tense translates 'had' done something. It uses the simple past form of ***haben/sein*** plus the past participle.
5. The pluperfect is very similar to the perfect tense.
6. The list on page 73 shows some past participles for using with the pluperfect tense.

Hast du's kapiert?

Look at Gramma's diary for next week. Write sentences to describe what she will be doing.

Am Montag wird sie 80 Bananen kaufen.

Grimmi was excluded from his last school. What had he done?

Frösche im Labor essen
Er hatte die Frösche im Labor gegessen

a im Musikunterricht schlafen
b nie Schuluniform tragen
c die Lehrer ärgern
d nie im Unterricht aufpassen
e immer frech sein
f immer spät zur Schule kommen

11 Modal verbs

- Modal verbs give extra meaning to a sentence. They help you to express yourself politely, to make requests, to give orders and advice and ask permission, as well as saying what you are able to do.

- There are six modal verbs in German:

  dürfen (to be allowed to)
  können (to be able to)
  mögen (to like)
  müssen (to have to)
  sollen (ought to)
  wollen (to want to)

- Modal verbs usually need an infinitive to complete their meaning:

Ich **kann** die Nase mit der Zunge **berühren**.	*I can touch my nose with my tongue.*
Sie **wollte** Karotten mit Schokosoße **essen**.	*She wanted to eat carrots with chocolate sauce.*
Er **muß** eine grüne Mütze zur Schule **tragen**.	*He has to wear a green cap to school.*

- A sentence with a modal verb works like a sentence in the future tense (⇨ p.76). The modal verb is the main verb in the sentence (⇨ p.94) and the infinitive goes at the end.

Grammar in action

Can you translate the cartoon strip?

Ich kann meine Hausaufgaben nicht machen

Ich muß meine Hausaufgaben machen

Ich will meine Hausaufgaben nicht machen

Du sollst deine Hausaufgaben machen

Du darfst jetzt deine Hausaufgaben machen

1 Modal verbs in the present tense

A All six modal verbs are irregular. They are mostly used in the present tense or the simple past.

B In the present tense the modal verbs go like this:

dürfen (to be allowed to)
ich darf
du darfst
er/sie/es darf
wir/sie/Sie dürfen
ihr dürft

Use ***dürfen*** to talk about things which people are/aren't allowed to do:

Man darf nicht fotografieren. *You aren't allowed to take photos.*

Man darf nicht rauchen. *You aren't allowed to smoke.*

Man darf hier parken. *You are allowed to park here.*

können (to be able to)
ich kann
du kannst
er/sie/es kann
wir/sie/Sie können
ihr könnt

Use **können** to talk about things which people can or cannot do:

Ein Pinguin kann nicht fliegen. — *A penguin can't fly.*
Frösche können sehr hoch springen. — *Frogs can jump very high.*
Das kann ich nicht. — *I can't do that.*

müssen (to have to)
ich muß
du mußt
er/sie/es muß
wir/sie/Sie müssen
ihr müßt

Use **müssen** to talk about things which people have to or don't have to do:

Wir müssen eine Uniform tragen. — *We have to wear a uniform.*
Er muß um acht Uhr zu Hause sein. — *He has to be at home at eight.*
Ich muß das nicht machen. — *I don't have to do that.*

wollen (to want to)
ich will
du willst
er/sie/es will
wir/sie/Sie wollen
ihr wollt

Use **wollen** to talk about things which people want or don't want to do:

Ich will Ärztin werden. — *I want to be a doctor.*
Wir wollen das Museum nicht besuchen. — *We don't want to visit the museum.*
Er will nicht. — *He doesn't want to.*

sollen (ought to)
ich soll
du sollst
er/sie/es soll
wir/sie/Sie sollen
ihr sollt

Use **sollen** to talk about things which people should or shouldn't do:

Wir sollen aufpassen. — *We should be careful.*
Ich soll nach Hause gehen. — *I should go home.*
Er soll dir nicht helfen. — *He shouldn't help you.*

mögen (to like)
ich mag
du magst
er/sie/es mag
wir/sie/Sie mögen
ihr mögt

Use **mögen** to talk about things which people like or don't like:

Ich mag Musik.	*I like music.*
Wir mögen Tennis.	*We like tennis.*
Er mag Katzen nicht.	*He doesn't like cats.*

☆ *The **ich** and **er/sie/es** forms of modal verbs are always the same. The **wir/sie/Sie** forms are the same as the infinitive and you don't use the **ihr** form very much, so there's not as much to learn as you think! Look at **wollen** and **sollen** – they are very similar.*

Test your understanding

Complete the following sentences.

Dagmar ..... nicht auf die Party ..... (wollen/gehen)
Dagmar will nicht auf die Party gehen.

a Meine junge Katze ..... zum Tierarzt ..... (müssen/gehen)
b Mein Papagei ..... sehr gut Deutsch ..... (können/sprechen)
c Im Zoo ..... man die Tiere nicht ..... (dürfen/füttern)
d ..... du in einem Zoo .....? (wollen/arbeiten)
e Du ..... Bienen nie ..... (sollen/töten)
f Mäuse ..... sehr gut ..... (können/hören)
g Unsere Hunde ..... immer im Park ..... (wollen/spielen)

Expand these sentences using ***darf (nicht)***, ***muß***, ***kann***.

Lachen verboten! – Man darf nicht lachen.

a Kauen verboten!
b Links fahren!
c Ohrringe erlaubt!
d Ruhig sein!
e Erwachsene im Kino verboten!
f Radio spielen verboten!
g Schuluniform tragen!

What are your school rules? Write them in German.
Man muß eine Uniform tragen. Man darf keine Ohrringe tragen .....

2 Simple past modals

A The lists below show you the modals in the simple past (note the lack of *umlauts* in this tense):

dürfen (to be allowed to)
ich durfte
du durftest
er/sie/es durfte
wir/sie/Sie durften
ihr durftet

Ich durfte in die Disco gehen. *I was allowed to go to the disco.*

können (to be able to)
ich konnte
du konntest
er/sie/es konnte
wir/sie/Sie konnten
ihr konntet

Sie konnte die Arbeit nicht machen. *She couldn't do the work.*

müssen (to have to)
ich mußte
du mußtest
er/sie/es mußte
wir/sie/Sie mußten
ihr mußtet

Er mußte Babysitting machen. *He had to babysit.*

sollen (ought to)
ich sollte
du solltest
er/sie/es sollte
wir/sie/Sie sollten
ihr solltet

Wir sollten nicht hereingehen. *We shouldn't go in.*

wollen (to want to)
ich wollte
du wolltest
er/sie/es wollte
wir/sie/Sie wollten
ihr wolltet

Ich wollte dieses Video nicht ausleihen. *I didn't want to hire this video.*

Test your understanding

Look at the class outing and say what happened.

Peter wollte nach Hause fahren.

3 könnte, möchte, würde

A These three modal forms are useful to learn:

- ***könnte*** (could)
- ***möchte*** (would like)
- ***würde*** (would).

B The examples below show how you can use these words.

Könnten Sie mir bitte **helfen**?	*Could you help me please?*
Könnte ich bitte hier **sitzen**?	*Could I sit here please?*

Er **möchte** ins Konzert **gehen**.	*He'd like to go to the concert.*
Ich **möchte** in die Karibik **fahren**.	*I'd like to go to the Caribbean.*
Ich **möchte** einmal Hamburger mit Pommes, bitte.	*I'd like a hamburger and chips, please.*
Mit dir **würde** ich nie **ausgehen**.	*I'd never go out with you.*
Würdest du gern ins Theater **gehen**?	*Would you like to go to the theatre?*

c The full forms go like this:

können (to be able to)
ich könnte
du könntest
er/sie/es könnte
wir/sie/Sie könnten
ihr könntet

mögen (to like)
ich möchte
du möchtest
er/sie/es möchte
wir/sie/Sie möchten
ihr möchtet

werden (to become)
ich würde
du würdest
er/sie/es würde
wir/sie/Sie würden
ihr würdet

Test your understanding

Can you say the following sentences in German?

a I'd like a hamburger please.
b Would you like to come to my party?
c I wouldn't help him.
d They could play with us.
e I wouldn't go there.
f Could I have a pen, please?
g We'd like to go to Japan.

4 *hätte, wäre*

A These two forms can be used as shown below:

Ich **hätte** gern einen Kaffee, bitte.	*I'd like a coffee please.*
Er **hätte** Angst.	*He'd be afraid.*
Das **wäre** gut.	*That would be good.*
Dann **wären** wir traurig.	*We'd be sad then.*

B They are often used with ***würde*** (would):

Wenn ich 1000 Mark **hätte**, **würde** ich feiern.	*If I had 1000 Marks, I'd celebrate.*
Wenn ich reich **wäre, würde** ich noch arbeiten.	*If I were rich, I'd still work.*
Was **würdest** du machen, wenn du kein Geld **hättest**?	*What would you do if you didn't have any money?*

C The complete forms are given below:

haben (to have)
ich hätte
du hättest
er/sie/es hätte
wir/sie/Sie hätten
ihr hättet

sein (to be)
ich wäre
du wärest
er/sie/es wäre
wir/sie/Sie wären
ihr wäret

Test your understanding

Complete these sentences.

Wenn ich Hunger ....., ... ich zu McDonalds ..... (haben/gehen)
Wenn ich Hunger hätte, würde ich zu McDonalds gehen.

a Wenn ich reich ....., ... ich einen BMW ..... (sein/kaufen).
b Wenn er Durst ....., ... er ein Mineralwasser ..... (haben/trinken).
c Wenn ich einsam ....., ... ich einen Freund ..... (sein/anrufen).
d Wenn wir Kinder ....., ... wir uns anders als unsere Eltern ..... (haben/benehmen).

Summary: Modal verbs

1 The six modal verbs in German are: **dürfen**, **können**, **mögen**, **müssen**, **sollen**, **wollen**.

2 The modal verbs usually need an infinitive to complete their meaning.

3 They are mainly used in the present tense and the simple past.

4 They are all irregular and must be learned separately.

5 In a sentence, the modal verb goes where the main verb normally goes and the infinitive goes at the end.

6 **könnte**, **möchte**, **würde**, **hätte** and **wäre** are useful forms for some phrases.

Make sentences about the Familie Gramm.

Der Hund/nicht bellen (dürfen) Der Hund darf nicht bellen.

a Graf Gramm/sich immer auf dem Dach duschen (wollen)

b Gräfin Gramm/zum Frühstück ein Glas Sekt trinken (sollen)

c Die Kinder/um Mitternacht ins Bett gehen (müssen)

d Die Katze/im Ofen schlafen (mögen)

e Der Briefträger/keine Rechnungen liefern (dürfen)

f Die Tür/immer auf sein (müssen)

g Das Baby/vier Sprachen sprechen (können)

Complete these sentences.

Stell dir vor, ...
du bist im Restaurant. Was hättest du gern? Ich hätte gern .....
du gewinnst 10 000 Mark. Was würdest du kaufen? Ich würde .....
du bist in Berlin. Was könntest du tun?
du hast den Nachmittag frei. Was möchtest du tun?
du kannst deine ideale Familie wählen. Was für Geschwister hättest du gern?
du darfst ein Land gratis besuchen. Wo würdest du hinfahren?

What differences are there between you now and when you were five? Describe the differences using the modal verbs, as in the examples below.

Mit fünf Jahren konnte ich nicht Rad fahren, aber jetzt kann ich gut Rad fahren.
Mit fünf Jahren wollte ich nie alleine sein, aber jetzt will ich oft alleine sein.

12 Word order

- Sentences are made up by placing a variety of words (i.e. nouns, adjectives, verbs and pronouns etc.) in a specific order.
- Every sentence begins with a capital letter and ends with a full stop.
- If the order of the sentence is wrong, the sentence is difficult to understand.

- Questions have a different order from statements.
- In German, some link words (i.e. ***weil***, ***daß***, ***wenn***, etc.) change the order of the sentence.

Grammar in action

Can you understand these jumbled headlines?

| spricht Hamster Unser Deutsch! |

sechs neue ist Jahre Fußballstar alt Der!

Kohl Kinder mehr essen immer!

illegal Hausaufgaben ist!

Now look at them in the right order.

Unser Hamster spricht Deutsch!
Der neue Fußballstar ist sechs Jahre alt!
Kinder essen immer mehr Kohl!
Hausaufgaben sind illegal!

1 Statements

A The most important thing about a German sentence is that the main verb comes as the second idea in the sentence.

Erdal	hatte	einen Hamster.
Am Montag	war	der Hamster krank.
Zwei Tage später	ist	der Hamster gestorben.
Jetzt	hat	Erdal eine Maus.

B In German, you don't always have to start the sentence with the person's name or a pronoun (***ich***, ***du***, ***er***, etc.). You can often start it with an expression of time but the verb must still be your second idea.

Wir **fliegen** immer erste Klasse.	*We always fly first class.*
Heute **fliegen** wir zweite Klasse.	*Today we're flying second class.*
Opa **spielt** Fußball.	*Grandad is playing football.*
Nächste Woche **spielt Opa** Badminton.	*Grandad is playing badminton next week.*
Um halb zwei **ist die Schule** aus.	*School finishes at half past one.*

Test your understanding

Write these sentences out. Always start with the underlined word.

C In a German sentence, the words are put in a certain order. To sort out the order, ask yourself: 1. When? 2. How? 3. Where?

- When? Any time details need to come first (**am Montag**, **um zehn Uhr**, **gestern**, ...)
- How? Further details come next (**mit dem Zug**, **schnell**, **eine rote Jacke**, ...)
- Where? Place words come at the end (**nach Ungarn**, **zur Schule**, **in der Stadt**, ...)

Am Montag fahre ich mit dem Zug nach Ungarn.	*I'm going to Hungary by train on Monday.*
Der Schüler läuft um zehn Uhr schnell zur Schule.	*At ten o'clock the pupil runs quickly to school.*
Gestern hat er eine rote Jacke in der Stadt gekauft.	*He bought a red jacket in town yesterday.*

D Remember that the verb still needs to be the second idea in the sentence.

E If you are using a past participle or a verb with an infinitive, they go right at the end.

F This chart shows you how German sentences are formed:

(1) When?	(2) Verb + Subject	(3) How?/What	(4) Where?
Am Dienstag	gehe ich	mit meiner Freundin	ins Kino.
Morgen	kauft Peter	eine Kassette	im Kaufhaus.

or

(1) Subject + Verb	(2) When?	(3) How?/What?	(4) Where?
Ich fahre	am Dienstag	mit dem Zug	nach Berlin.
Ich lese	immer	sehr gern	zu Hause.

Test your understanding

Can you put these sentences in the right order?

a die Katze im Wohnzimmer Gestern *war* **krank**.
b in den Dschungel ich *Im Mai* fahre mit meiner Mutter.
c **interessiert sich** *Olaf* **für Briefmarken** gar nicht.

d im Kino *Am Donnerstag* **gibt es** *einen guten Film.*
e ***Jeden Tag* Tennis** spielt Joachim im Sportzentrum.
f **gehen wir** Übermorgen in die Schule **nicht**.
g ***mit ihrer Klasse*** **Meike fährt** *in die Berge.*

▲▲▲

2 Questions

A You can ask a question by putting the verb first in the sentence and changing the intonation of your voice:

Du gehst in die Stadt.	*You're going to town.*
/**Gehst du** in die Stadt?	*/You're going to town?*
Er spielt Fußball.	*He plays football.*
/**Spielt er** Fußball?	*/He plays football?*
Sie wohnen in Amerika.	*They live in America.*
/**Wohnen sie** in Amerika?	*/They live in America?*

B You can also use ***nicht wahr?*** at the end of a statement to change it into a question:

Du bist intelligent, **nicht wahr?**	*You're clever, aren't you?*
Er spielt gut, **nicht wahr?**	*He plays well, doesn't he?*
Sie haben schreckliche Kinder, **nicht wahr?**	*They've got terrible children, haven't they?*

C To ask other kinds of questions, you need to use a question word. This list shows the main ones:

was? (what?)	Was machst du am Montag?
was für? (what kind/sort?)	Was für ein Auto habt ihr?
wann? (when?)	Wann kommst du nach Großbritannien?
warum? (why?)	Warum hast du kein Geld?
welche(r/s)? (which?)	Welches Hemd findest du schöner?
wer? (who?)	Wer ist dein bester Freund?
wie? (how?)	Wie schreibt man dein Name?
wieviel? (how much?)	Wieviel kostet das?
wie viele? (how many?)	Wie viele Mädchen gibt es in deiner Klasse?
wo? (where?)	Wo wohnst du?
woher? (from where?)	Woher kommst du?
wohin? (to where?)	Wohin gehst du heute abend?
worüber? (about what?)	Worüber redet ihr?
wen? (who? – accusative)	An wen schreibst du?

wem? (who? – dative)	Mit wem gehst du ins Kino?
wessen? (whose?)	Wessen Schuh ist das?

Two useful phrases worth learning are:

Wieviel Uhr ist es?	*What's the time?*
Wie bitte?	*Pardon?*

D The word order for a question is:

(Question Word)	Verb/ Subject	When/How/Where	(Verb/pp)
Was	machst du	am Montag in der Stadt?	
Wer	hat dir	gestern	geholfen?
Was	wird sie	nächstes Jahr	machen?
Worüber	lachst du?		
Warum	gehst du	immer	schwimmen?
	Kommt ihr	morgen vorbei?	
	Ist er	oft zum Arzt	gegangen?

Test your understanding

Turn these statements into questions.

Er spielt Squash. Spielt er Squash?/Er spielt Squash, nicht wahr?

a Wir lernen Deutsch.
b Das ist eine Katze.
c Sie essen zu viel Schokolade.
d Wir haben viele Hausaufgaben.
e Sie sieht wunderbar aus.
f Er geht oft ins Kino.
g Der Witz war lustig.

Match the questions and the answers.

a Wo wohnst du?
b Wie viele Brüder hast du?
c Gehst du in die Schule?
d Wann hast du Geburtstag?
e Wer ist dein Lehrer?
f Was ißt du zum Frühstück?
g Warum lachst du?

Der Witz ist lustig **Toast** **11.05** **Hameln**
4 **ja** **Herr Thomas**

Here are some answers. Can you write the questions?

Ich wiege 50 Kilo. – Wieviel wiegst du?

a Ich lese einen Krimi.
b Meine Stadt liegt in der Nähe von Rostock.
c Sie heißt Renate.
d Er kommt aus der Türkei.
e Das kostet acht Mark.
f Es ist acht Uhr dreißig.
g Klaus kommt mit.

Write ten questions to ask your partner. Can your partner answer them?

1. Wie heißt die Hauptstadt von Italien?
2. Wieviel wiegt ein Tennisball?
3. Wie heißt 'umbrella' auf deutsch?

▲▲

3 *und, aber, sondern, oder, denn*

A If you use ***und*** (and), ***aber*** (but), ***sondern*** ('but' in negative sentences), ***oder*** (or), ***denn*** (because) to link two halves of a sentence, the order stays the same as normal.

Mustafa spielt Gitarre**, und** seine Schwester singt sehr gern.
Mustafa plays the guitar and his sister likes singing.
Ich wohne in Bonn**, aber** ich arbeite in Dresden.
I live in Bonn but I work in Dresden.
Ich wohne nicht in Bodenheim**, sondern** in Bobenheim.
I don't live in Bodenheim, but in Bobenheim.
Er geht gern in die Kneipe**, denn** die Getränke sind billig.
He likes going to the pub because the drinks are cheap.
Gehen wir ins Theater**, oder** bleiben wir hier?
Shall we go to the theatre or shall we stay here?

B When you are joining two sentence halves together, remember to put a comma before the joining word (**,aber ,denn ,oder ,sondern**).

C ***und*** only has a comma if the second part of the sentence has a subject pronoun (***ich***, ***du***, ***er***, ...) or name in it.

Er spielt Tennis**, und** Claudia hört Musik.
He plays tennis and Claudia listens to music.

Er spielt Tennis **und** findet es anstrengend.

He plays tennis and finds it tiring.

Claudia hört Musik **und** ißt Schokolade.

Claudia listens to music and eats chocolate.

Test your understanding

Complete the sentences.

a An einem Schultag stehe ich früh auf(,) und .....
b Am Wochenende gehe ich in die Stadt, oder .....
c Meine Familie ist sehr nett, aber .....
d Ich gehe gern in die Schule, denn .....
e Ich bin kein Sportfan, sondern .....

4 *weil, daß, ...*

A ***weil*** (because) and ***daß*** (that) link two halves of a sentence. With conjunctions like these, the second verb goes to the end of the clause.

Ich gehe gern in die Schule**, weil** meine Freunde dort **sind**.

I like going to school because my friends are there.

Meine Eltern sind böse**, weil** ich furchtbare Noten **habe**.

My parents are angry because I've got dreadful grades.

Ich weiß**, daß** wir nach Köln **ziehen**.

I know that we're moving to Cologne.

Es freut mich**, daß** du **gekommen bist**. *I'm glad that you've come.*

B Here are some other conjunctions like ***weil*** and ***daß***:

- ***wenn*** if, whenever, when (present tense)

Es ist traurig**, wenn** ich nach Hause **gehen muß**.

It's sad when I have to go home.

Wenn es **regnet, bleibe** ich zu Hause.

Whenever it rains, I stay at home.

Wenn ich spät **ankomme, gibt** es sicher Ärger.

If I'm late, there's bound to be trouble.

☆ *Look at the order of the sentence when the conjunction is at the beginning. The verb after it goes to the end of the first half, and then there is a comma followed by the verb from the second half.*

- ***als*** when (past tenses)

Als er jung **war, trug** er breite Hosen.

When he was young he wore flared trousers.

Es **regnete** stark**, als** wir angekommen sind.

It was raining hard when we arrived.

- ***sobald*** as soon as

Sobald ich sechzehn **bin, verlasse** ich die Schule.

As soon as I'm sixteen, I'll leave school.

Ich war froh**, sobald** wir wieder zu Hause waren.

I was happy as soon as we were home again.

- ***obwohl*** although

Obwohl ich klein **bin, kann** ich schnell laufen.

Although I'm small, I can run fast.

Er lachte**, obwohl** er sehr krank war.

He laughed, although he was very ill.

- ***nachdem*** after

Nachdem die Katze verschwunden **ist, kauften** wir eine Schildkröte.

After the cat disappeared, we bought a tortoise.

Er hat zu viel getrunken**, nachdem** er die neue Stelle bekam.

He drank too much after he got his new job.

- ***bevor*** before

Bevor du auf Urlaub **fährst, mußt** du mir deine Adresse geben.

Before you go on holiday, you must give me your address.

Ich habe zwei Stunden gewartet**, bevor** sie angekommen ist.

I waited two hours before she arrived.

- ***während*** while

Während du hier **bist, kannst** du mir helfen.

While you're here you can help me.

Ich stricke**, während** ich den Film sehe.

I'm knitting while watching this film.

☆ *Notice how a comma comes before conjunctions like **weil** and **daß**. You will score marks if you remember to use one.*

Test your understanding

Rewrite these sentences using the words given in brackets.

Ich kann nichts hören. Sie spielt die Musik zu laut. (weil)
Ich kann nichts hören, weil sie die Musik zu laut spielt.

a Das Hemd ist schrecklich. (weil) Es ist sehr altmodisch.
b (obwohl) Deutsch ist schwierig. Es ist auch interessant.
c (wenn) Das Wetter ist wolkig. Es regnet sofort.
d Es stimmt. (daß) CDs sind besser als Kassetten.
e Ich lese ein Buch. (während) Du spielst Tennis.
f Der Mann sah den Dieb. (als) Er kam nach Hause.
g Monika geht zum Strand. (sobald) Sie kann schwimmen.

Work with a partner. Say a sentence. Can your partner continue your sentence using one of the conjunctions from this section?

A: Ich spiele gern Tennis,
B: weil ich Tennisfan bin.
B: Ich gehe gern in die Schule,
A: wenn wir Sport haben .....

5 *zu, um ..... zu*

A These phrases use ***zu*** with an infinitive:

Ich **habe Lust**, ins Kino **zu** gehen.	*I want to go the cinema.*
Er **versucht** Deutsch **zu** lernen.	*He's trying to learn German.*
Ich **hoffe**, dich bald wieder **zu** sehen.	*I hope to see you soon.*
Es ist einfach, Deutsch **zu** lernen.	*It's easy to learn German.*
Sie **fängt an zu** weinen.	*She's starting to cry.*

B ***um ..... zu*** translates 'in order to do' something:

Ich fahre nach Österreich, **um** mein Deutsch **zu** verbessern.
I'm going to Austria to improve my German.

Mein Bruder geht joggen, **um** fit **zu** bleiben.
My brother goes jogging in order to keep fit.

Um Lehrer(in) **zu** sein, muß man lang studieren.
In order to be a teacher you have to study for a long time.

Test your understanding

Write these sentences with ***um ..... zu***.

Er fährt nach Prag. Warum? Er will seine Freundin besuchen.
Er fährt nach Prag, um seine Freundin zu besuchen.

a Er spart Geld. Warum? Er will einen CD-Spieler kaufen.
b Wir bleiben zu Hause. Warum? Wir müssen eine Torte backen.
c Du gehst zum Sportzentrum. Warum? Du willst Volleyball spielen.
d Sie geht zur Kneipe. Warum? Sie will Leute kennenlernen.
e Er schreibt an seinen Brieffreund. Warum? Er will sein Deutsch verbessern.

6 Separable verbs

A Separable verbs are verbs such as ***fernsehen*** (to watch TV), ***abwaschen*** (to wash up), ***zumachen*** (to close). In these verbs there is a short word (often a preposition) at the start of the infinitive.

B Separable verbs split up when you use them in a sentence. The first part of the verb goes to the end of the sentence. The main part of the verb goes as the second idea in the sentence.

Jeden Abend **sieht** mein Hund viel **fern**.	*My dog watches a lot of TV every evening.*
Unser Papagei **wäscht** sehr oft **ab**.	*Our parrot often washes up.*
Die Katze **macht** die Tür nie **zu**.	*The cat never closes the door.*

C If you are using separable verbs in the perfect tense, you put the **ge-** between the two parts of the verb to make the past participle: ***ferngesehen abgewaschen zugemacht.***

Hast du dein Zimmer **aufgeräumt**?	*Have you tidied up your room?*
Ich habe alles schon **eingepackt**.	*I've already packed everything.*
Das hat erst gestern **angefangen**.	*That only started yesterday.*

D If you use a separable verb with a modal verb or a conjunction, the separable verb goes together at the end of the clause.

Ich muß meinen Freund **anrufen**.	*I must ring my friend.*
Ich wollte alleine **skifahren**.	*I wanted to ski on my own.*

Wenn du alles **mitnimmst**, mußt du extra zahlen.
If you take everything with you, you'll have to pay extra.

Test your understanding

Describe these pictures.

fernsehen im Wohnzimmer   Ich sehe im Wohnzimmer fern.

a abwaschen mit meinem Freund

b skifahren in Österreich

c einsteigen ins Auto

d radfahren mit meiner Familie

e aufpassen auf unsere Schlange

Write sentences to explain what these people did yesterday.

Gestern hat Paul Zeitungen ausgetragen.

PAUL	Zeitungen austragen
SONJA	ihr Zimmer aufräumen
RAINER	Getränke vom Markt abholen
EMINE	das Essen vorbereiten
VALERIE	ihre Freunde anrufen
SILVIO	im Wald spazierengehen
BENEDIKT	an einen Wettbewerb teilnehmen

Summary: Word order

1 The key thing to remember in a German sentence is that the main verb comes as the second idea in the sentence.

2 The general order of a sentence is: When? How? Where?

3 You can ask a question with a small question word, or you can swap round the order of the verb and the subject.

4 Words like ***aber***, ***denn***, ***und***, ***oder***, ***sondern*** don't change the order of the sentence.

5 Conjunctions like ***weil*** and ***daß*** change the order of the sentence.

6 Some verbs use ***zu***, and ***um ..... zu*** means 'in order to'.

7 Separable verbs have a small word (often a preposition) at the beginning, which often separates from the main verb in a sentence.

Hast du's kapiert?

Can you write out the muddled sentences in the correct order?

a doof finde Film diesen ich.

b du Banane eine hast?

c ins mache Theater ich ein Nachmittagsschläfchen gehe und.

d mit an fahren die Küste Montag dem Hubschrauber wir am.

e zu machen einen Kopfstand ich versuche.

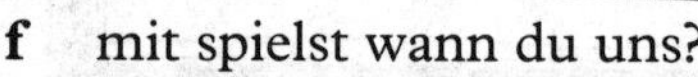

f mit spielst wann du uns?

g brav, ich aufgeräumt bin die Küche habe weil ich.

Can you write .....

5 questions with question words
4 questions without question words
3 sentences with separable verbs
2 sentences with ***daß***
1 sentence with a separable verb and ***weil***?

What about your partner? See who can write them first, and then compare what you have written.

Can you complete these sentences?

a Ich gehe (nicht) gern in die Schule, weil .....
b Sobald ich sechzehn bin, ...
c Ich finde es schön, wenn .....
d Als ich acht Jahre alt war, ...
e Obwohl ich nur Teenager bin, ...
f Wenn wir unsere Umwelt retten wollen, ist es wichtig, daß .....

13 Numbers

1 *eins, zwei, drei, ...*

A Here are the German numbers:

- 1–10

1 eins
2 zwei (**zwo** is occasionally used to avoid confusion between **zwei** and **drei**, e.g. on the phone)
3 drei
4 vier
5 fünf
6 sechs
7 sieben
8 acht
9 neun
10 zehn

- 11–19

11 elf
12 zwölf
13 dreizehn
14 vierzehn
15 fünfzehn
16 sechzehn
17 siebzehn
18 achtzehn
19 neunzehn

- 20–29

20 zwanzig
21 einundzwanzig
22 zweiundzwanzig
23 dreiundzwanzig
24 vierundzwanzig
25 fünfundzwanzig
26 sechsundzwanzig
27 siebenundzwanzig
28 achtundzwanzig
29 neunundzwanzig

- 30–100

30 dreißig
40 vierzig
50 fünfzig
60 sechzig
70 siebzig
80 achtzig
90 neunzig

30 to 90 all follow the pattern of 20:
35 = fünfunddreißig (five and thirty)
46 = sechsundvierzig (six and forty)

☆ ***When you hear a number between 21 and 99, write it from right to left as you will always hear the second number first.***

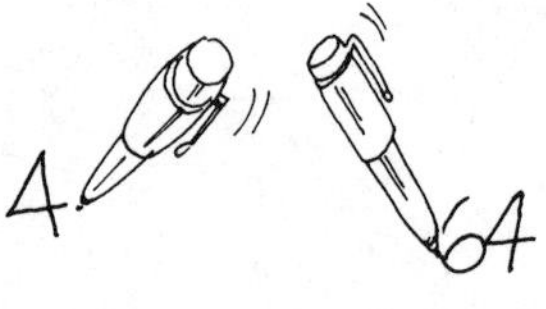

- higher numbers

100 = (ein)hundert
250 = zweihundertfünfzig
375 = dreihundertfünfundsiebzig
1 000 = (ein)tausend
2 319 = zweitausenddreihundertneunzehn

Do not put ***und*** after the words ***tausend*** or ***hundert***.

B Numbers are always written as one word. Some numbers can make very long words: 5 672 = fünftausendsechshundertzweiundsiebzig!

C In German you do not add a comma to separate numbers above thousands, but a space instead: 12 500 (12,500 in English).

D To say the year, put all the numbers together as one long word:

1996 = neunzehnhundertsechsundneunzig
2031 = zweitausendeinunddreißig

☆ *You can usually write large numbers as figures – 127 or 8 734 – so you don't need to worry too much about the spelling.*

Test your understanding

Say these numbers and carry on the pattern as far as you can.

2, 4, 6, 8, ... zwei, vier, sechs, acht, zehn, ...

a 3, 6, 9, 12, ...
b 21, 31, 41, 51, ...
c 100, 150, 200, 250, ...
d 5, 10, 15, 20, ...
e 2, 4, 16, 256, ...
f 1 091, 2 092, 3 093, 4 094, ...
g 36 000, 18 000, 9 000, 4 500, ...

2 *erste, zweite, dritte .....*

A These numbers are called ordinal numbers. You use them for dates (***den ersten Mai***/May the first) and positions in a list (***das sechste Mal***/the sixth time).

☆ *In English we use 'st' (1st), 'rd' (3rd) and 'th' (4th) to show an ordinal number, but in German you just add a full stop after the number: 1. 3. 4.*

B To say 1st–19th in German you add ***-te*** to the normal number. There are a few exceptions to this:

1. der **erste**
2. der zwei**te**
3. der **dritte**
4. der vier**te**
5. der fünf**te**
6. der sechs**te**
7. der **siebte**
8. der ach**te**
9. der neun**te**
10. der zehn**te** .....
17. der siebzehn**te** .....
19. der neunzehn**te**

C For numbers from 20th you add ***-ste*** to the normal number:

20. der zwanzig**ste**
21. der einundzwanzig**ste**
22. der zweiundzwanzig**ste**

30. der dreißig**ste** .....
90. der neunzig**ste**
100. der hundert**ste**

D When an ordinal number comes before a noun, it works like an adjective and sometimes needs an ending (⇨ pp.29–31):

Heute ist der elfte März.	*Today is the eleventh of March.*
Am elfte**n** März.	*On the eleventh of March.*
Zum sechste**n** Mal.	*For the sixth time.*

Test your understanding

Say these dates out loud.

6. Februar – am sechsten Februar

a 11. Mai
b 29. Juli
c 22. November
d 24. Februar
e 17. August
f 5. Dezember
g 30. Januar

3 Useful numbers

A Prices are written:

0,80 DM (achtzig Pfennig)
12,45 DM (zwölf Mark fünfundvierzig)
90,80 ÖS (neunzig Schilling achtzig)
12,30 SF (zwölf Franken dreißig)

B Telephone numbers are usually split into groups of two figures: 23 54 21. They are spoken in three groups: dreiundzwanzig, vierundfünfzig, einundzwanzig.

C Distances and weights need numbers:

80 cm (achtzig Centimeter)
50 m (fünfzig Meter)
100 km (hundert Kilometer)
30 l (dreißig Liter)
80 g (achtzig Gramm)
45 kg (fünfundvierzig Kilogramm)

D Dates need numbers: 12.08.98 (zwölften, achten, achtundneunzig).

E If you are saying the year, you can either say the numbers on their own, or ***im Jahre 2000***.

Ich bin zweitausendeins geboren. *I was born in 2001.*
Im Jahre zweitausendeins bin ich geboren.

F You need the numbers for telling the time (⇨ p.111).

Summary: Numbers

1 There are two types of numbers:
- ***eins, zwei, drei*** ..... (cardinal numbers)
- ***erste, zweite, dritte*** ..... (ordinal numbers)

2 Larger numbers are all written as one word.

Ask and answer these questions with a partner.

a Wie alt bist du?
b Was ist deine Telefonnummer?
c Was ist deine Lieblingszahl?
d Was ist dein Geburtsdatum?
e Wie viele Schüler(innen) gibt es in deiner Klasse?
f Was ist das Datum heute?
g Wie viele Zähne hast du?

Say these sentences with the numbers.

14 Time

1 The 24-hour clock

A The 24-hour clock is used a lot in Germany. Once you know your numbers (⇨ p.105) it is easy – you simply say the numbers with **Uhr** in the middle:

09.56 = neun Uhr sechsundfünfzig
14.50 = vierzehn Uhr fünfzig
24.00 = vierundzwanzig Uhr (Mitternacht)

B To say 'at' with a time, use ***um***:

Es beginnt **um** achtzehn Uhr fünf.	*It starts at 18.05.*
Gehen wir **um** acht Uhr fünfundvierzig?	*Shall we go at 08.45?*
Der Zug fährt **um** sechzehn Uhr drei ab.	*The train leaves at 16.03.*

☆ *As with the numbers, you rarely need to spell times out, but you do need to know how to say them.*

Test your understanding
Say these times out loud.

18.05 – um achtzehn Uhr fünf

a 21.50
b 03.45
c 15.34
d 12.59
e 07.00
f 13.21
g 24.09

2 The 12-hour clock

A The 12-hour clock follows a similar pattern to English:

Viertel vor sechs	*quarter to six*
zehn nach drei	*ten past three*
sieben Uhr	*seven o'clock*

B The main thing to remember is that in English you say half *past* the hour but in German you say half *to* the *next* hour:

halb acht = half past seven (i.e. half an hour to eight)
halb drei = half past two (i.e. half an hour to three)

C This clock shows you all the expressions you need for the 12-hour clock:

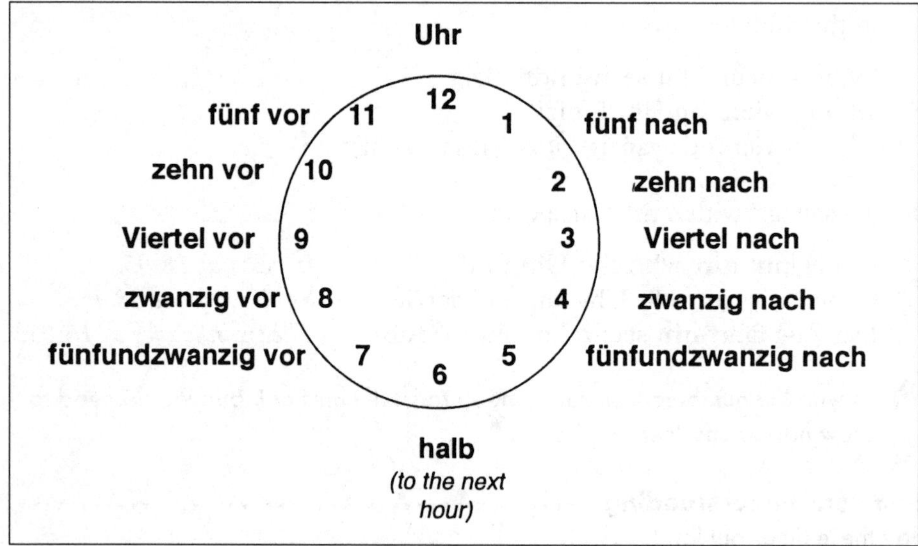

D To say 'at' with a time, use ***um***:

Es beginnt **um** fünf nach sechs.	*It starts at five past six.*
Gehen wir **um** Viertel vor neun?	*Shall we go at quarter to nine?*

E Here are some useful time questions:

Wieviel Uhr ist es?	*What's the time?*
Um wieviel Uhr beginnt der Film?	*What time does the film start?*
Wann fährt der Zug ab?	*When does the train leave?*

Test your understanding

Say these times out loud.

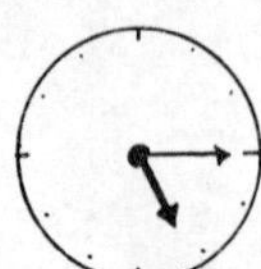

Es ist Viertel nach fünf.

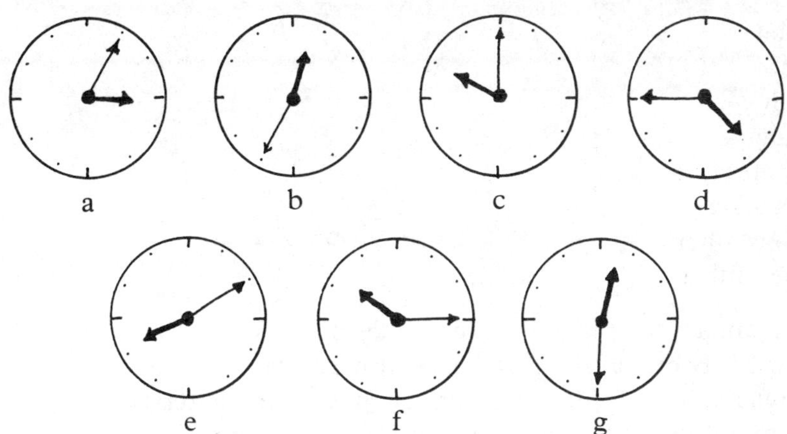

Describe a typical school day.

Um Viertel vor sieben wache ich auf. Um zehn vor sieben stehe ich auf .....

3 Useful time expressions

A ***die Woche*** (the week)

Montag
Dienstag
Mittwoch
Donnerstag
Freitag
Samstag/Sonnabend
Sonntag

am Montag	(on Monday)
montags	([on] Mondays)
jeden Montag	(every Monday)
Montagvormittag	(Monday morning)
Montagnachmittag	(Monday afternoon)
Montagabend	(Monday evening)

B ***das Jahr*** (the year)

Januar
Februar
März
April

Mai
Juni
Juli
August
September
Oktober
November
Dezember

im Januar	(in January)
am 14. Februar	(on February 14)
Freitag, den 13. Juli	(Friday, July 13 [on letters])
vom 6. Juni bis 8. Juli	(from June 6 to July 8)

c Here are some useful time phrases:

heute	(today)
heute abend	(tonight)
heute morgen	(this morning)
heute früh	(early today)
am Morgen	(in the morning)
morgens	(in the mornings)
am Abend	(in the evening)
abends	(in the evenings)
jeden Tag	(every day)
jedes Wochenende	(every weekend)
jedes Jahr	(every year)
letzte Woche	(last week)
letztes Jahr	(last year)
morgen	(tomorrow)
übermorgen	(the day after tomorrow)
nächste Woche	(next week)
nächstes Jahr	(next year)
gestern	(yesterday)
vorgestern	(the day before yesterday)
gestern vormittag	(yesterday morning)
gestern nachmittag	(yesterday afternoon)
gestern abend	(yesterday evening)

Test your understanding

Translate these into German.

a on Saturday
b from March 5 to April 21
c at six o'clock
d last year
e on Sundays
f in December
g on May 25

Summary: Time

1 The 24-hour clock is used a lot in German and it is easy to say.

2 The 12-hour clock follows the English pattern, apart from half past the hour, which in German indicates half to the next hour.

3 The days of the week and the months are similar to English.

Answer these questions.

- **a** Wann hast du Geburtstag?
- **b** Wann stehst du auf?
- **c** Wieviel Uhr ist es jetzt?
- **d** An welchen Tagen hast du Deutsch in der Schule?
- **e** Wann beginnt die Schule?
- **f** Wann bist du geboren?
- **g** Wann siehst du fern?

15 Grammar checklist quiz

Talking about things

a What is a noun? (⇨ p.1)
b What are the three genders in German? (⇨ p.1)
c How do you make a plural noun? (⇨ p.4)
d What are the four cases? (⇨ p.9)
e How do ***der***, ***die***, ***das*** change in the cases? (⇨ p.9)
f When do you use the nominative case? (⇨ p.10)
g When do you use the accusative case? (⇨ p.12)
h When do you use the dative case? (⇨ p.13)
i When do you use the genitive case? (⇨ p.14)
j Which prepositions always take the accusative case? (⇨ p.20)
k Which prepositions always take the dative case? (⇨ p.20)
l Which prepositions take either the accusative or the dative case? (⇨ p.20)
m How do you decide if you use the accusative or the dative case for the prepositions in **l**)? (⇨ p.21)
n What is an adjective? (⇨ p.28)
o What endings do adjectives need after der, die, das (⇨ p.29)
p What endings do adjectives need after ein, eine, ein (⇨ p.30)
q How do you compare two things in German? (⇨ p.33)
r How do you say something is the biggest/fastest/hardest etc? (⇨ p.34)

Talking about people

a What are the different ways of saying 'you'? (⇨ p.41)
b When do you use ***er***, ***sie*** or ***es***? (⇨ p.40)
c When do you use accusative pronouns? (⇨ p.42)
d What are the accusative pronouns? (⇨ p.43)
e What are the dative pronouns? (⇨ p.44)
f How do you say 'who/which' (relative pronouns)? (⇨ p.45)

Talking about actions

a What is a verb? (⇨ p.50)
b What is the pattern for a regular verb in the present tense? (⇨ p.52)
c How are ***haben*** and ***sein*** formed in the present tense? (⇨ p.55)
d What are the three ways of giving a command? (⇨ p.56)

- **e** What is a reflexive verb? (⇨ p.57)
- **f** What is the perfect tense? (⇨ p.60)
- **g** How do you form the perfect tense? (⇨ p.60)
- **h** How do you form regular past participles? (⇨ p.61)
- **i** When do you use the simple past? (⇨ p.68)
- **j** How do you form the simple past for regular verbs? (⇨ p.68)
- **k** How do you form the future tense? (⇨ p.76)
- **l** How do you form the pluperfect? (⇨ p.78)
- **m** What are the six modal verbs? (⇨ p.81)
- **n** What do ***könnte***, ***möchte***, ***hätte***, ***wäre*** and ***würde*** mean? (⇨ p.86)

Asking and giving information

- **a** Where does the verb come in a sentence? (⇨ p.93)
- **b** What is the order of a sentence? (⇨ p.94)
- **c** How can you ask a question without a question word? (⇨ p.95)
- **d** How many question words do you know? (⇨ p.95)
- **e** What do ***weil***, ***daß*** and ***wenn*** do to a sentence? (⇨ p.98)
- **f** What does ***um ..... zu*** mean? (⇨ p.100)
- **g** Can you name five separable verbs? (⇨ p.101)
- **h** What happens to a separable verb? (⇨ p.101)
- **i** Can you count to 1000? (⇨ p.105)
- **j** Can you say 1st to 100th? (⇨ p.107)
- **k** How do you use the 24-hour clock? (⇨ p.111)
- **l** How do you use the 12-hour clock? (⇨ p.111)

Answers

1 Nouns

Grammar in action p.1
Fruchtmilch (fruit milk), Früchte (fruit), Erdbeeren (strawberries), Bananen (bananas), Milch (milk), Gabel (fork), Teller (plate), Milchtopf (milk jug), Mixer (mixer)

Test your understanding
1 p.2
(m) der: Goldfisch, Hamster, Papagei, Hund
(f) die: Kuh, Katze, Schlange, Schildkröte
(n) das: Pony, Pferd, Kaninchen, Krokodil

a die Freundin = *female friend*
b der Mittwoch = *Wednesday*
c das Österreich = *Austria*
d die Biologie = *Biology*
e der Honig = *honey*
f das Europa = *Europe*
g die Sekretärin = *secretary*
h der Nachbar = *male neighbour*
i die Karriere = *career*

2 p.3
a eine Orange = *an orange*
b ein Kiwi = *a kiwi*
c eine Banane = *a banana*
d eine Erdbeere = *a strawberry*
e ein Pfirsich = *a peach*
f ein Obst = *a piece of fruit*

3 p.4
a Bettzeug (n) = *bed covers*
b Tischtennis (m) = *table tennis*
c Kleingeld (n) = *change*
d Zahnärztin (f) = *female dentist*
e Fotoapparat (n) = *camera*
f Schlafanzug (m) = *pyjamas*
g Kühlschrank (m) = *fridge*

a das Bett = *bed*; das Zeug = *thing*
b der Tisch = *table*; der Tennis = *tennis*

c klein = *small;* das Geld = *money*
d der Zahn = *tooth;* die Ärztin = *female doctor*
e das Foto = *photo;* das Apparat = *machine*
f der Schlaf = *sleep;* der Anzug = *suit*
g kühl = *cool;* der Schrank = *cupboard*

4 p.5
a der Sohn/die Söhne
b die Tante/die Tanten
c das Mädchen/die Mädchen
d der Freund/die Freunde
e die Nichte/die Nichten
f das Kind/die Kinder
g die Schwiegertochter/die Schwiegertöchter

p.6
a die Szene/die Szenen
b die Schublade/die Schubladen
c der Pickel/die Pickel
d das Geschenk/die Geschenke
e das Jugendhaus/die Jugendhäuser
f das Interview/die Interviews
g das Theaterstück/die Theaterstücke

Hast du's kapiert? p.7
(m): Graf, Keller
(f): Familie, Schule, Gräfin, Schlittschuhdisco
(n): Schloß, Deutschland, Schwimmbad, Leben
(pl): Kinder, Jahre, Eltern, Partys, Feste, Spiele, Freunde

p. 8
das Kleid, ein Kleid, die Kleider, *dress(es)/clothes*
die Socke, eine Socke, die Socken, *sock(s)*
das Hemd, ein Hemd, die Hemden, *shirt(s)*
der Mantel, ein Mantel, die Mäntel, *coat(s)*
der Rock, ein Rock, die Röcke, *skirt(s)*
das T-Shirt, ein T-Shirt, die T-Shirts, *T-shirt(s)*
die Krawatte, eine Krawatte, die Krawatten, *tie(s)*
der Anzug, ein Anzug, die Anzüge, *suit(s)*
die Hose, eine Hose, die Hosen, *trouser(s)*

a ein (the others are all nouns)
b Briefträger (the others are all feminine)

c Fähre (the others are all neuter)
d Hand (the others are all masculine)
e Banane (the others are all plural)
f Phantasie (the others are all compound nouns)

2 Cases

Test your understanding

1 p.11

a Kühe
b Sie
c Das Brot
d der Briefträger
e Der Kaffee
f ich
g die Schule

2 p.12

a den Teller
b den Kerl
c den Dom
d die Sehenswürdigkeiten
e die ganze Familie
f Den Film
g die Kinder

3 p.14

a der
b dem
c dem
d den
e dem
f der

4 p.15

a Das Lieblingsessen der Katzen ist Milchpudding.
b Das Lieblingsessen des Hundes ist Schokosoße.
c Das Lieblingsessen der Maus ist Käsebrot.
d Das Lieblingsessen des Pferds ist Müsli.
a Das Auto des Fahrers ist schnell.
b Die Bluse der Lehrerin ist altmodisch.
c Der Schnurrbart des Stars ist dumm.
d Die Kekse der Kinder sind lecker.

5 p.16

a meinem
b einer
c Ihre
d Deine
e keinen
f Seine
g eine

Hast du's kapiert? p.17

a eine
b Mein
c mein/einen
d einen
e Die/unserer/den

p.18

a Ich helfe dem Arzt/der Ärztin.
b Das Mädchen erzählt den Kindern eine Geschichte.
c Der Junge dankt der Polizistin.
d Meine Schwester zeigt der Klasse ihre Fotos.
e Reichst du bitte dem Gast das Salz?
f Wir geben den Katzen Schokolade.
g Wir zeigen dem Kind unsere Karte.

3 Prepositions

Grammar in action p.19

nach = *to,* bis = *until,* ab = *from,* für = *for,* auf = *on,* gegenüber = *opposite*

Test your understanding

1 p.21

a durch
b mit
c von/zu
d für
e um
f aus
g Um

a dem
b den
c der
d einen
e meinen
f deinem
g der

2 p.23

a der (dat.)
b dem (dat.)
c die (acc.)
d meinem (dat.)
e die (acc.)
f der (dat.)
g dem (dat.)

a Ich lege die Bücher auf das Regal. Jetzt sind die Bücher auf dem Regal.
b Ich stecke das Geld in die Tasche. Jetzt ist das Geld in der Tasche.
c Ich hange das Bild an die Wand. Jetzt hängt das Bild an der Wand.

d Der Hund kriecht unter das Bett. Jetzt schläft der Hund unter dem Bett.
e Sie läuft vor das Kino. Er wartet vor dem Kino.
f Ich arbeite in der Bäckerei. Jeden Tag gehe ich in die Bäckerei.

3 p.25
a Man ißt damit.
b Man arbeitet damit.
c Man sieht damit.
d Man spielt damit.

Hast du's kapiert? p.26
Das Radio ist in der Küche. Die Töpfe sind im Schlafzimmer. Die Kleider sind im Wohnzimmer und der Fernseher ist im Badezimmer. Das Geschirr ist im Flur, und die Blumen sind in der Garage. Die Brille seiner Oma ist im Kühlschrank!

4 Adjectives

Grammar in action p.28
hübsch, blond, angeberisch, nett, freundlich, hilfsbereit, blonden

Test your understanding
1 p.30
a der neue Tunnel
b das scheußliche Wetter
c die wahnsinnigen Erwachsenen
d diese stinklangweilige Autobahnstrecke
e alle freundliche Österreicher
f jede interessante Sprache
g Welche gemeine Witze?

2 p.31
a Ich möchte eine tolle Kassette.
b Ich habe einen bunten Teller.
c Das ist ein guter Computer.
d Ist das deine neue Uhr?
e Siehst du seine junge Kinder?
f Gibt es ein interessantes Programm heute abend?
g Du bist ein furchtbarer Junge.

3 p.32
schwarze Schuhe, gestreifte Krawatte, karierte Hose, schwarzer Pulli, weiße Jacke

4 p.34
leicht/schwer
alt/jung
schnell/langsam
einfach/schwierig
kurz/lang
faul/fleißig
klein/groß
teuer/billig

a Bonbons sind teuerer als Schokolade. Schokolade ist billiger als Bonbons.
b Karl ist schwerer als Margit. Margit ist leichter als Karl.
c Der Kuli ist länger als der Stift. Der Stift ist kürzer als der Kuli.
d Dirks Auto ist langsamer als Gabis. Gabis Auto ist schneller als Dirks.
e Birgit ist fleißiger als Jörg. Jörg ist fauler als Birgit.
f Mathe ist schwieriger als Geschichte. Geschichte ist einfacher als Mathe.
g Felix ist größer als Eleni. Eleni ist kleiner als Felix.

5 p.36
Der längste Fluß ist der Nil.
Das kürzeste Wort ist O!
Der höchste Berg ist Everest.
Das schnellste Tier ist der Gepard.
Die kleinste Münze ist 1 Pfennig.

Hast du's kapiert? p.38
große, beste, leckere, modische, schöne, neue, häßliche, karierte, neue, gutes, freundliche

5 Personal pronouns

Grammar in action p.39
Ihre, wir, uns
We're standing up for your health.

Test your understanding
1 p.42
a Was liest du gern?
b Was lesen Sie gern?
c Was lesen Sie gern?
d Was liest du gern?
e Was lest ihr gern?
f Was liest du gern?
g Was liest du gern?

a Er
b Wir
c sie
d Es
e er
f es

2 p.43

a es
b sie
c sie
d euch
e sie
f ihn
g sie

3 p.44

a mir
b ihm
c ihnen
d ihr
e ihr
f euch
g uns

4 p.46

a Sie heißt Susanna.
b Er heißt Hansi.
c Es heißt Michael.
d Er heißt Norbert.
e Er heißt Bruno.
f Sie heißt Uli.
g Es heißt Dorothee.

p.47

a ein Einzelkind
b ein Rollstuhl
c ein Haustier
d ein Mädchen
e die Schule/Universität
f die Deutschen
g das Badezimmer

Hast du's kapiert? p.48

ich/mich/mir; du/dich/dir; er/ihn/ihm; sie/sie/ihr; es/es/ihm; wir/uns/uns; Sie/Sie/Ihnen; ihr/euch/euch

Heute spiele ich Basketball mit meinen Freunden. Wir spielen einmal in der Woche. Wir spielen unten im Keller. Es macht uns Spaß! Nach dem Spiel gehen meine Freunde zurück in die Stadt. Ich aber nicht. Ich besuche dann meine Freundin. Sie wohnt in einem Wohnblock. Er ist neben unserem Park. Wir gehen zusammen ins Eiscafé. Normalerweise ist es sehr romantisch. Leider kommen manchmal Gramma und ihre Freundinnen ins Eiscafé. Sie ärgern mich sehr. Sie sitzen am Tisch. Dann bestellen sie Eis, und sie kichern. Grisilde und ich verlassen dann das Eiscafé. Wir gehen im Park spazieren. Dorthin kommt Gramma nicht, weil sie gegen die Parkbäume allergisch ist.

6 Verbs

Grammar in action p.50
fahren = *to drive,* sein = *to be,* überholen = *to overtake,* kommen = to *come,* versuchen = *to try,* vermeiden = *to avoid*

Test your understanding

2 p.52

a ich höre, du hörst, er hört, wir/sie hören, ihr hört
b ich mache, du machst, er macht, wir/sie machen, ihr macht
c ich sage, du sagst, er sagt, wir/sie sagen, ihr sagt
d ich renne, du rennst, er rennt, wir/sie rennen, ihr rennt
e ich studiere, du studierst, er studiert, wir/sie studieren, ihr studiert
f ich rufe, du rufst, er ruft, wir/sie rufen, ihr ruft
g ich klettere, du kletterst, er klettert, wir/sie klettern

a machst
b spielt
c Hört
d springen
e angeln
f wohnen
g liebe

3 p.54

a finde
b ißt
c Sprechen
d fährst
e Seht
f nehme
g gibt

sehe, spricht, arbeitet, geht, nimmt, gibt, fällt, läuft, steht, steigt, fährt, folgen

4 p.55

a Ich bin schlecht gelaunt.
b Sie sind sehr sympatisch.
c Ich habe Kopfschmerzen.
d Wir haben einen neuen Computer.
e Hast du deine Jacke?
f Sie hat keine Freunde.
g Ihr seid sehr frech.

5 p.56

a Mach einen Kopfstand!
b Zeichnet ein schönes Bild!
c Sing ein Lied!
d Stehen Sie auf einem Bein!
e Sei nicht so frech!
f Zahlen Sie bis hundert!
g Kitzelt eure Partner!

6 p.57

a sich
b uns
c euch
d sich
e dich
f mich
g sich

Hast du's kapiert? p.59
folgen, hat, kommt, ist, hat, trägt, erreichen, fährt, ist, regnet, hält, steigt, machen, rufe, Sind, antwortet, bin, habe, Nehmen

7 The perfect tense

Grammar in action p.61
habe verloren (have lost)
haben gesehen (have seen)

Test your understanding

1 p.62

a gestellt (put) – stellen (to put)
b gelacht (laughed) – lachen (to laugh)
c gekauft (bought) – kaufen (to buy)
d geklatscht (clapped) – klatschen (to clap)
e geplaudert (chatted) – plaudern (to chat)
f aufgepaßt (looked after; watched out) – aufpassen (to look after; watch out)
g telefoniert (phoned) – telefonieren (to phone)

a Mozart hat in Salzburg gewohnt.
b Beckenbauer hat Fußball gespielt.
c Einstein hat die Relativitätstheorie entdeckt.
d Die Brüder Grimm haben viele Märchen erzählt.
e Gustav Klimt hat Bilder gemalt.
f Marlene Dietrich hat oft Theater gespielt.
g Karl Benz hat das erste Auto hergestellt.

2 p.64

a gemacht/gedacht
b gekommen/genommen
c getrunken/gestunken
d getrieben/geblieben
e gelesen/gewesen
f gesprochen/gebrochen
g gesungen/gesprungen

a geben (to give) – gegeben (given)
b gehen (to go) – gegangen (gone)
c beginnen (to begin) – begonnen (begun)
d treiben (to do) – getrieben (done)
e trinken (to drink) – getrunken (drunk)
f denken (to think) – gedacht (thought)
g schlafen (to sleep) – geschlafen (slept)

3 p.66

a 1989 ist die Mauer hingefallen.
b 1969 ist ein Mann zum Mond geflogen.
c 1990 hat Deutschland die Fußballweltmeisterschaft gewonnen.
d 1960 haben Frauen in der Schweiz das Wahlrecht bekommen.
e 1916 ist Franz Josef gestorben.
f 1865 hat Wagner *Tristan und Isolde* geschrieben.
g 1945 ist der Zweite Weltkrieg zu Ende gegangen.

Hast du's kapiert? p.67

Sie hat eine Froschsuppe gekocht. Sie ist in die Wasserdisco gegangen. Sie hat mit Oma Gramm telefoniert. Sie hat tausend Mark ausgegeben. Sie hat eine Mütze gestrickt. Sie hat Grimmi geärgert.

8 The simple past

Grammar in action p.68

One mile. Four minutes.
On May 6 1954 it was cool and windy. A lot of people gathered on the Iffley Road Track in Oxford. Among them was the young English medicine student, Roger Bannister. He was wearing white shorts and a white T-shirt. His goal was to run a mile in four minutes. He reached his goal in three minutes 59.4 seconds. There was a new world record.

Test your understanding

1 p.69

spielte, regnete, machte, hörten, schauten, beobachteten, weinte, lachte, lachte, versuchte, erreichte, suchte, kletterte, erreichte, kratzte, lächelte

2 p.70
a gewann – gewinnen (to win)
b lag – liegen (to lie)
c nahm – nehmen (to take)
d ließ – lassen (to leave)
e sang – singen (to sing)
f sprach – sprechen (to speak)
g verlor – verlieren (to lose)

a trug
b lebten
c arbeiteten
d gab
e konnte
f schien
g war

Hast du's kapiert? p.72
war, ging, schickte, machte, steckte, sang, wollte, kam, hatte, konnte, fand, mußte

10 Other tenses

Test your understanding

1 p.77
a aber nächste Woche werde ich wieder fit sein.
b aber nächstes Jahr wird er auf die Uni gehen.
c aber am Wochenende werde ich eine Party haben.
d aber das nächste Spiel werden wir gewinnen.
e aber heute abend wirst du viele Hausaufgaben haben.
f aber nächste Woche wird sie Karten spielen.
g aber im nächsten Jahrhundert werden wir mit dem Elektromofa fahren.

2 p.78
a Florian hatte den Bus verpaßt.
b Thomas und Xavier hatten einen Unfall gehabt.
c Mehmet war krank gewesen.
d Joachim war zum Arzt gegangen.
e Nina hatte Kopfschmerzen gehabt.
f Kai und sein Bruder hatten ihre Sportsachen verloren.
g Lisa und Markus waren einkaufen gegangen.

Hast du's kapiert? p.79
Am Dienstag wird sie 20 km schwimmen.
Am Mittwoch wird sie die Schule schwänzen.
Am Donnerstag wird sie 10 Filme sehen.

Am Freitag wird sie in die Stadt fahren.
Am Samstag wird sie ein Buch schreiben.
Am Sonntag wird sie im Bett bleiben!

p.80

a Er hatte im Musikunterricht geschlafen.
b Er hatte nie Schuluniform getragen.
c Er hatte die Lehrer geärgert.
d Er hatte nie im Unterricht aufgepaßt.
e Er war immer frech gewesen.
f Er war immer spät zur Schule gekommen.

11 Modal verbs

Grammar in action p.81

I can't do my homework. I've got to do my homework. I don't want to do my homework. You've got to do your homework. You may now do your homework.

Test your understanding

1 p.84

a Meine junge Katze muß zum Tierarzt gehen.
b Meine Papagei kann sehr gut Deutsch sprechen.
c Im Zoo darf man die Tiere nicht füttern.
d Willst du in einem Zoo arbeiten?
e Du sollst Bienen nie töten.
f Mäuse können sehr gut hören.
g Unsere Hunde wollen immer im Park spielen.

a Man darf nicht kauen!
b Man muß links fahren!
c Man darf Ohrringe tragen!
d Man muß ruhig sein!
e Erwachsene dürfen nicht ins Kino gehen!
f Man darf das Radio nicht spielen!
g Man muß Schuluniform tragen!

2 p.86

Helenka konnte nicht sehr gut schwimmen!
Claudia mußte auf Erwin aufpassen.
Die Klasse durfte keinen Kaugummi essen.
Erdal sollte im Schatten sitzen.
Oli und Frank wollten Feuer machen.
Sabine mußte aufs Klo!
Alle dürften ein Bier trinken.

3 p.87

a Ich möchte einen Hamburger, bitte.
b Möchtest du auf meine Party kommen?
c Ich würde ihm nicht helfen.
d Sie könnten mit uns spielen.
e Dort würde ich nicht hingehen.
f Könnte ich bitte einen Kuli haben?
g Wir möchten nach Japan fahren.

4 p.88

a Wenn ich reich wäre, würde ich einen BMW kaufen.
b Wenn er Durst hätte, würde er ein Mineralwasser trinken.
c Wenn ich einsam wäre, würde ich einen Freund anrufen.
d Wenn wir Kinder hätten, würden wir uns anders als unsere Eltern benehmen.

Hast du's kapiert? p.89

a Graf Gramm will sich immer auf dem Dach duschen.
b Gräfin Gramm soll zum Frühstück ein Glas Sekt trinken.
c Die Kinder müssen um Mitternacht ins Bett gehen.
d Die Katze mag im Ofen schlafen.
e Der Briefträger darf keine Rechnungen liefern.
f Die Tür muß immer auf sein.
g Das Baby kann vier Sprachen sprechen.

12 Word order

Grammar in action p.92

Unser Hamster spricht Deutsch!
Der neue Fußballstar ist sechs Jahre alt!
Kinder essen immer mehr Kohl!
Hausaufgaben sind illegal!

Test your understanding

1 p.93

a Ich habe Heimweh.
b Jeden Tag schreibe ich an meine Eltern.
c Meine Eltern telefonieren nicht.
d Ich kaufe Kekse und Schokolade.
e Ich habe ein Mädchen getroffen.
f Meine neue Freundin heißt Katja.
g Wir gehen zusammen in die Disco.

p.94

a Gestern war die Katze krank im Wohnzimmer.
b Im Mai fahre ich mit meiner Mutter zum Dschungel.
c Olaf interessiert sich gar nicht für Briefmarken.
d Am Donnerstag gibt es einen guten Film im Kino.
e Jeden Tag spielt Joachim Tennis im Sportzentrum.
f Übermorgen gehen wir nicht in die Schule.
g Meike fährt mit ihrer Klasse in die Berge.

2 p.96

a Lernen wir Deutsch? Wir lernen Deutsch, nicht wahr?
b Ist das eine Katze? Das ist eine Katze, nicht wahr?
c Essen sie zu viel Schokolade? Sie essen zu viel Schokolade, nicht wahr?
d Haben wir viele Hausaufgaben? Wir haben viele Hausaufgaben, nicht wahr?
e Sieht sie wunderbar aus? Sie sieht wunderbar aus, nicht wahr?
f Geht er oft ins Kino? Er geht oft ins Kino, nicht wahr?
g War der Witz lustig? Der Witz war lustig, nicht wahr?

a Hameln
b 4
c ja
d 11.05
e Herr Thomas
f Toast
g Der Witz ist lustig.

a Was liest du?
b Wo liegt deine Stadt?
c Wie heißt sie?
d Woher kommt er?
e Was kostet das?
f Wieviel Uhr ist es?
g Wer kommt mit?

4 p.99

a Das Hemd ist schrecklich, weil es sehr altmodisch ist.
b Obwohl Deutsch schwierig ist, ist es auch interessant.
c Wenn das Wetter wolkig ist, regnet es sofort.
d Es stimmt, daß CDs besser als Kassetten sind.
e Ich lese ein Buch, während du Tennis spielst.
f Der Mann sah den Dieb, als er nach Hause kam.
g Monika geht zum Strand, sobald sie schwimmen kann.

5 p.100

a Er spart Geld, um einen CD-Spieler zu kaufen.
b Wir bleiben zu Hause, um eine Torte zu backen.
c Du gehst zum Sportzentrum, um Volleyball zu spielen.
d Sie geht zur Kneipe, um Leute kennenzulernen.
e Er schreibt an seinen Brieffreund, um sein Deutsch zu verbessern.

6 pp.101–103
a Ich wasche mit meinem Freund ab.
b Ich fahre in Österreich ski.
c Ich steige ins Auto ein.
d Ich fahre mit meiner Familie rad.
e Ich passe auf unsere Schlange auf.

Sonja hat ihr Zimmer aufgeräumt.
Rainer hat Getränke vom Markt abgeholt.
Emine hat das Essen vorbereitet.
Valerie hat ihre Freunde angerufen.
Silvio ist im Wald spazierengegangen.
Benedikt hat an einen Wettbewerb teilgenommen.

Hast du's kapiert? p.104
a Ich finde diesen Film doof.
b Hast du eine Banane?
c Ich gehe ins Theater und mache ein Nachmittagsschläfchen.
d Am Montag fahren wir mit dem Hubschrauber an die Küste.
e Ich versuche einen Kopfstand zu machen.
f Wann spielst du mit uns?
g Ich bin brav, weil ich die Küche aufgeräumt habe.

13 Numbers

Test your understanding

1 p.107
a drei, sechs, neun, zwölf
b einundzwanzig, einunddreißig, einundvierzig, einundfünfzig
c hundert, hundertfünfzig, zweihundert, zweihundertfünfzig
d fünf, zehn, fünfzehn, zwanzig
e zwei, vier, sechzehn, zweihundertsechsundfünfzig
f tausendeinundneunzig, zweitausendzweiundneunzig, dreitausenddreiundneunzig, viertausendvierundneunzig
g sechsunddreißigtausend, achtzehntausend, neuntausend, viertausendfünfhundert

2 p.108
a am elften Mai
b am neunundzwanzigsten Juli
c am zweiundzwanzigsten November
d am vierundzwanzigsten Februar
e am siebzehnten August
f am fünften Dezember
g am dreißigsten Januar

Hast du's kapiert? p.110

a neunundzwanzig
b zwölf, vierunddreißig, sechsundfünfzig
c hundertsiebzehn
d zweitausenddrei
e dreihundertvierundsiebzigtausendsechshundertachtundfünfzig
f dreizehnten
g fünften

14 Time

Test your understanding

1 p.111

a einundzwanzig Uhr fünfzig
b drei Uhr fünfundvierzig
c fünfzehn Uhr vierunddreißig
d zwölf Uhr neunundfünfzig
e sieben Uhr
f dreizehn Uhr einundzwanzig
g vierundzwanzig Uhr neun

2 p.113

a fünf nach drei
b fünfundzwanzig vor eins
c zehn Uhr
d Viertel vor fünf
e zehn nach acht
f Viertel nach zehn
g halb eins

3 p.115

a am Samstag
b vom fünften März bis den einundzwanzigsten April
c um sechs Uhr
d letztes Jahr
e sonntags
f im Dezember
g am fünfundzwanzigsten Mai

Hast du's kapiert? p.115

Wieviel Uhr ist es?
Um halb acht.
Am Montag oder heute?
Aber der Film beginnt um acht Uhr vierundvierzig.
Heute abend habe ich nichts vor.